The WetFeet Insider Guide to Industries and Careers for MBAs

2004 Edition

Helping you make smarter career decisions.

WetFeet Inc.

609 Mission Street
Suite 400
San Francisco, CA 94105

Phone: (415) 284-7900 or 1-800-926-4JOB
Fax: (415) 284-7910
E-mail: info@wetfeet.com
Website: www.wetfeet.com

The WetFeet Insider Guide to Industries and Careers for MBAs

ISBN: 1-58207-259-0

Table of Contents

Introduction 1

Industries 3

Biotechnology & Pharmaceuticals 4

Commercial Banking 13

Computer Hardware 20

Computer Software 26

Consulting 32

Consumer Electronics 41

Consumer Products 47

Energy & Utilities 55

Enterprise Software 63

Entertainment & Sports 69

Health Care 77

Internet & New Media 83

Investment Banking 90

Mutual Funds & Brokerage 99

Networking & Peripherals 107

Nonprofit & Government 113

Real Estate 121

Semiconductors 128

Telecommunications 134

Venture Capital. 141

Careers 149

Asset Management. 150

Business Development. 156

Consulting 160

Corporate Finance 167

General Management. 173

Investment Banking. 180

Marketing. 186

Operations 191

Project Management 196

Securities Sales & Trading 199

Introduction

The purpose of this guide is to provide you with a broad range of information about careers and industries, so that you can consider a full range of career options available to MBAs.

The guide is divided into two sections. The first section provides information about a variety of industries that hire MBAs, from biotechnology to venture capital. These Industry Profiles will give you an idea of what's going on in various industries, as well as opportunities that may be available within them and companies that may be most likely to offer those opportunities. Most of these Industry Profiles contain descriptions of jobs specific to the industries in which MBAs might make a good fit. Be aware that, in addition to those jobs specified, just about every industry will offer opportunities in the standard corporate functions: marketing, operations, finance, and so on. The second section provides more information about a variety of career functions, from business development to project management, which you will find across a range of industries.

This guide is an initial resource to help you in your career management process. You can access additional information for each industry and career function by going to WetFeet.com. Other industries and careers are also listed on the site, including advertising, accounting, retail, and more. In each section, other Web-based resources are listed to help you learn more. Please let us know how this guide has helped you, and send us any suggestions, to comments@wetfeet.com.

Good luck!

Industries

WetFeet®

Biotechnology & Pharmaceuticals

Industry Overview

Pharmaceutical companies produce and market drugs, from familiar over-the-counter compounds like aspirin to exotic prescriptions that inhibit, activate, or otherwise affect individual molecules involved in specific medical conditions. They also produce livestock feed supplements, vitamins, and a host of other products. America's pharmaceutical industry is consistently one of the most profitable in the United States. The drug business is booming: Globally, the industry sells more than $300 billion worth of drugs each year.

Biotechnology is a relatively new kid on the block. Simply put, biotechnology, the applied knowledge of biology, seeks to duplicate or change the function of a living cell so it will work in a more predictable and controllable way. The biotechnology industry uses advances in genetics research to develop products for human diseases and conditions. Several biotech companies also use genetic technology to other ends, like the manipulation of crops.

Biotech opportunities largely mirror those in the pharmaceutical industry. The key difference is that biotech firms are much more focused on research because they are still developing their initial products. Marketing and sales forces grow when—and if—a viable product nears FDA approval. This means that jobs for nonscientists are scarcer in biotech than in pharmaceuticals.

This is an industry with a potent and promising future. Demand for drugs is growing, fueled by an aging global population and blossoming international markets—Europe, Latin America, and especially Asia are the hot regions. The industry has maintained growth rates nearly double those of the economy at large and is expected to maintain that performance well into the next decade. But take note: Anybody with a genuine interest in pharmaceuticals or biotech should get acquainted with the details of the industry mergers that have occurred in the past decade.

Trends

Biotech alliances. Because the cost of soup-to-nuts drug development, manufacturing, marketing, and sales is prohibitive, a growing number of biotech companies that once dreamed of competing on equal terms with "Big Pharma," the handful of multinational giants that dominate the industry, now instead seek partnerships. Indeed, in the first three quarters of 2001, biotech companies took in $1.9 billion through such deals, an increase of 14 percent over the same period in 2000.

The nature of these alliances varies: In some instances, a biotech shop exchanges an exclusive license to market and sell a patented drug to a pharmaceutical company that is willing to pay some research costs up front. Such agreements may also include limited use of the pharmaceutical company's manufacturing and distribution channels.

In other instances, a pharmaceutical company makes a cash investment in exchange for a portion of future revenues and/or an equity stake in the biotech partner. This type of relationship is often tied to a marketing and distribution deal like the one described above. As a result, it's not unusual for Big Pharma to have biotech holdings that give them a substantial piece of the action.

Consolidation. Big Pharma and biotech alike are in the throes of long-range, large-scale consolidation. "Where there were 200 companies ten years ago, there are now 40," says one insider, "and by 2003 those 40 will become ten. It will be like the auto industry, where a small handful of players dominates the global marketplace." In 2002, Amgen bought Immunex, and in 2003, Pfizer purchased Pharmacia for $54 billion, making Pfizer the third-largest U.S. drug maker. Since economies of scale are often a significant factor in mergers and acquisitions, the consolidation trend can have a negative impact on the number of jobs available in the industry.

Expiring patents and weak pipelines. Why so much recent consolidation? One reason is that patents are expiring on a significant number of blockbuster drugs such as Prozac and Claritin, and many companies are lacking much of promise in their new-product pipelines. When patents expire, the market is opened to competition from lower-priced generic versions of the drugs. Sales can drop by as much as 80 percent. In response, many companies try to develop and market drugs that are similar to their blockbusters with expiring patents. For instance, Eli Lilly tried to compensate for the loss of Prozac revenue, when that drug's patent expired, by introducing a one-dose-per-week version of the drug, and Schering-Plough is following up its Claritin drug with a new, similar drug called Clarinex. Companies also try to increase the amount of time their blockbusters are patent-protected via legal defenses of their patents, delaying the date when generic versions of their drugs can go to market. Finally, companies look to shore up their product pipelines through mergers and acquisitions, or by signing pacts with biotechs.

Human genome map. The human genome is the sum total of all of the genes that exist in humans—over 100,000. In June 2000, after a bitter race to map the human genome, the federally funded Human Genome Project and the biotech firm Celera set aside their rivalry and announced that they had completed a "working draft." Meanwhile, private organizations such as Human Genome

Sciences and Incyte Genomics continue to conduct their own research on the human genome because they can patent commercial uses for every gene that they are the first to sequence and identify in terms of function.

Though skeptics have suggested that genomics work is overhyped, the industry consensus is that it will quickly usher in an era in which we can design and manufacture "rational drugs" that interface perfectly with the body's cellular receptors and yield maximal therapeutic benefits without unfavorable side effects or drug interactions.

Bioethics and stem cell research. Except for red blood, sperm, and egg cells, every cell in the human body contains a full set of genes. Each adult cell is dedicated to one specific function, such as a muscle, nerve or skin cell. Human embryos however, contain stem cells, which have the capacity to develop in virtually any way. Stem cell technology could allow scientists to generate new organs as an alternative to organ donation and provide human tissue for drug development and testing. But because stem cells are only found in human embryos, a storm of debate has arisen surrounding the ethics of biotechnology research.

In the summer of 2001, President Bush announced a new federal policy to allow stem cell research on already existing embryos developed for the purpose through in vitro fertilization. With federal endorsement on its side, stem cell research could become the next revolution in biotechnology.

Troubles in pharma and biotech land. All the news isn't rosy in the land of biotech and pharma. Weak new-product pipelines, in addition to the general economic downturn, have depressed stock prices. In addition, the industry is taking a lot of criticism over its profit margins. Protesters are questioning the morality of insisting on huge profit margins for AIDS drugs when hundreds of thousands of people in Third World countries have AIDS but can't afford

treatment. Closer to home, there's political pressure on pharma companies to lower prescription-drug prices for people in programs like Medicaid.

How It Breaks Down

Big Pharma. The handful of multinational giants that dominate the industry, known to insiders as Big Pharma, employs tens of thousands of people and sell drugs in every corner of the world. The majority are headquartered in this country, but several are based in Western Europe—particularly Switzerland, Germany, and France. Those headquartered in the United States are all located east of the Mississippi—the greatest concentration of home offices stretches along the corridor between Philadelphia and northern New Jersey.

Given the chance, people tend to work at these companies for decades rather than years, as there are abundant opportunities for dynamic careers in every field. In general, life is stable and lucrative: Big Pharma companies take an average of 30 cents in profit for each dollar they get in revenue—twice the margin in most industries. The fly in the ointment is an ongoing wave of mergers and alliances, a trend that will continue to shape the industry, the number of Big Pharma companies, and employment in years to come.

Diversified versus nondiversified Big Pharma. Big Pharma companies can be divided into two categories: diversified and nondiversified. In addition to developing and selling prescription drugs, diversified outfits—like Johnson & Johnson—maintain a wide array of other healthcare-related businesses, such as medical device companies or consumer health product divisions.

Nondiversified operations—like Merck—focus solely on the development and sale of drugs. (Not all such drugs are for humans—Pfizer, widely viewed as one of the most shrewdly operated companies in the business, takes in more than $1 billion every year in revenues from its animal health division.)

Among diversified companies, the current thinking favors divesting nonpharmaceutical concerns and focusing on the drug business, which tends to be leaner and more profitable. A heads-up to job seekers who go to work for a nonpharmaceutical division in a diversified company with hopes of getting a foot in the pharmaceutical door: You may wake up one morning to find your job spun off from the parent company.

Biotech. Despite the decline of the stock market, and the current general economic malaise, biotech concerns continue to attract investment dollars. Indeed, biotech is one of the few sectors that consistently receives infusions of VC capital in the current economic environment.

Despite the success of such biotech giants as Amgen and Genentech, a large majority of biotech shops are still small enough for everyone to know everyone else's name. Many biotechs are still in start-up phases, often with single, usually unproven, technologies and no products on (or sometimes even near) the market.

But a growing number of companies are joining an elite group of biotech firms—such as Biogen, Genzyme, Gilead Sciences, and Protein Design Labs— that have received FDA product approval and are in various stages of commercialization. Most jobs in smaller biotech firms are scientific, but these companies also have opportunities in marketing, manufacturing, engineering, and sales. Culturally, even the largest biotechs are more like tiny biotech shops—with leaner, flatter organizations—than like Big Pharma.

Many biotech firms have partnered up with Big Pharma in an effort to shore up cash reserves through the long drug-development process. These deals can take a variety of forms, but often the larger firm underwrites the smaller one's research in exchange for distribution rights, some portion of future profits, or another combination of privileges. Check into a company's list of partnerships to better understand what you're signing up for.

Key Jobs for MBAs

A note about salaries: At large pharmaceutical companies, people in management positions earn significant bonuses in cash and stock options. At many biotech companies, all employees receive stock options, which, if the company does well, can be lucrative. These bonuses are not reflected in the salary ranges below.

Marketing analyst/associate product manager. Job seekers without backgrounds in science can find work on the marketing side in Big Pharma and large biotech companies. A marketing analyst is primarily responsible for coordinating and implementing campaigns for specific drugs and/or audiences. Many MBAs enter the industry this way, and—perhaps more important—few without MBAs move far beyond the marketing analyst level, although this varies from company to company.

Salary range: $35,000 to $75,000.

Product manager. This job requires managing a team of people and working to determine price, distribution, brand image, forecasting, and overall strategy for one or more drugs. On a micro level, the job can be claustrophobic—imagine spending 13 months of six-day weeks learning every aspect of a single drug, then having the company decide that it would be best simply to let the product die. But over the years you should be exposed to some of the most important, dynamic, and profitable drug markets in the industry—an experience that will give you a synoptic overview and make you a greater asset to the company.

Salary range: $60,000 to $100,000

Key Biotech and Pharmaceutical Companies by 2002 Revenue

Company	Revenue ($M)	% Change from 2001	# of Employees
Merck	51,790	9	62,000
Johnson & Johnson	36,298	10	108,300
Pfizer	32,373	0	98,000
GlaxoSmithKline	31,819	7	100,000
Aventis	21,659	6	91,729
Novartis	19,335	−11	71,116
Bristol-Myers Squibb	18,119	0	44,000
Abbott Laboratories	17,685	9	71,819
Roche Group	15,638	−12	63,717
Wyeth	14,584	3	52,762
Eli Lilly	11,078	0	43,700
Schering-Plough	10,180	4	30,500
Amgen	5,523	47	10,100
Genentech	2,252	8	5,252
Barr Laboratories	1,189	133	1,075
Applera Corp.	1,701	4	6,000
Serono	1,547	12	n/a
Genzyme Corp.	1,330	9	5,600
Watson Pharmaceuticals	1,223	5	3,729
Biogen	1,148	10	2,633
Amersham Biosciences	1,075	9	4,400
Chiron Corp.	973	−15	4,044
Invitrogen	649	3	2,744

Sources: Fortune.com; Hoovers.com; WetFeet analysis.

Industries

WetFeet®

Additional Resources

Bio.com (http://www.bio.com)

BioView (http://www.bioview.com)

Hoover's Biotechnology Industry Snapshot
(http://www.hoovers.com/industry/snapshot/profile/0,3519,9,00.html)

Hoover's Pharmaceuticals Industry Snapshot
(http://www.hoovers.com/industry/snapshot/profile/0,3519,32,00.html)

InPharm.com (http://www.inpharm.com/)

Knowledge @ Wharton: Health Economics
(http://knowledge.wharton.upenn.edu/category.cfm?catid=6)

McKinsey Quarterly: Health Care
(http://www.mckinseyquarterly.com/category_editor.asp?L2=12)

Pharmaceutical Online
(http://www.pharmaceuticalonline.com/content/homepage/default.asp)

Commercial Banking

Industry Overview

Asked why he robbed banks, Willie Sutton replied, "Because that's where the money is." That was in the '30s, but even today, despite changes, a lot of the money is still in commercial banks. Most of us maintain checking accounts at commercial banks and use their ATMs. The money we deposit in our neighborhood bank branch or credit union supports local economic activity through small business loans, mortgages, auto loans, and home repair loans. The bank also provides loans in the form of credit card charges, and it renders local services including safe deposit, notary, and merchant banking. The bank branch or credit union office remains the cornerstone of Main Street economic life.

Trends

Consolidation and new jobs. For decades, banks profited by simply holding customers' money and charging them check writing fees and interest on loans. Jobs were well defined and stable, and promotion paths were clear and secure. Not anymore. Consolidation, competition, and technological change are shaking the industry to its core, forcing layoffs but also creating opportunity.

Since 1995, more than 200 large and small banks have merged. Several of these and a handful of recently consolidated giants—Citigroup, Bank of America, Bank One—dominate the banking industry. The new behemoths are entering new markets, while at the same time closing branches and replacing service personnel with online and other technologies. However, hiring by a growing number of nonbanks compensates for this trend to a degree. These firms, which

are pioneering new ways of delivering financial services, include MBNA and Capital One, which are credit card lenders; transaction processing and data services like First Data and Fiserv; and bill-payment-services marketers like MFSDC and Integrion.

Deregulation. The Glass-Steagall bill, passed by Congress in 1933, served as the backbone of banking regulation. During the late '90s, however, banks and other financial institutions found ways around the restrictions placed on them by Glass-Steagall and related legislation. Finally, in late 1999, Glass-Steagall was repealed, eliminating the legal framework for Depression-era boundaries that had already been abandoned by large financial services firms, including banks.

In theory, the repeal of Glass-Steagall opened the floodgates to consolidation, spawning superfirms that will offer banking, insurance, and securities. However, big firms are already doing this through affiliated companies—Citigroup, for example, offers insurance through its Travelers subsidiary—so the impact of the Glass-Steagall repeal remains to be seen.

Problem loans and lower profits. The recent spate of corporate accounting misdeeds, and the resulting bankruptcy of some companies, means that some banks are stuck trying to recoup loans from corporations that are cash-starved. On the consumer side of the business, in January 2002, 4.9 percent of all home loans were past due, a full point higher than a year earlier. And the average household has $8,000 in credit card debt, up from $3,000 in 1990. In the current economic environment, banks' performance could get even worse.

How It Breaks Down

As a job seeker, the most important distinction to keep in mind is between regional banks and the big global ones. Here we've broken down the industry by type of banking, rather than size of player, since banks are increasingly adding new services to their array of traditional ones.

Consumer or retail banking. This is what most people think of when they think of banking: A small to midsized branch with tellers and platform officers—the men and women in suits sitting at the nice wooden desks with pen sets—to handle customers' day-to-day needs. Although thousands of small community banks, credit unions, and savings institutions still exist, employment opportunities are increasingly coming from a few megaplayers such as Citibank, Bank of America, and Bank One, most of which seem hell-bent on building national—and even international—banking operations.

One complicating factor in this picture is that the banks mentioned above, in addition to extending their consumer-banking operations, have added to their portfolios by strengthening their investment-banking and asset-management capabilities, among others. So, if you want to work at a Citibank branch, make sure that you're applying to the right part of the organization.

Business or corporate banking. Many of the players in this group are the same ones in the consumer-banking business; others you'll find on Wall Street, not Main Street. At the highest level, the larger players (Bankers Trust, Bank of New York, and J.P. Morgan Chase & Co. being three names to add to the list of megaplayers above) provide a wide range of advisory and transaction-management services to corporate clients. Depending on which institution and activity area you join, the work can resemble branch banking or investment banking.

Securities and investments. Traditionally, this field has been the domain of a few Wall Street firms. However, as federal regulations have eased, many of the biggest commercial banks, including Bank of America, Citibank, J.P. Morgan Chase & Co., and others, have aggressively added investment-banking and asset-management activities to their portfolios. For people interested in corporate finance, securities underwriting, and asset management, many of these firms offer an attractive option. However, the hiring for these positions will frequently be done separately from that for corporate and consumer banking.

Nontraditional options. Increasingly, a number of nonbank entities are offering opportunities to people interested in financial services. Players include credit card companies such as American Express, MasterCard, and Visa; credit card issuers like Capital One and First USA; and credit-reporting agencies such as TRW. Although people at these firms are still in the money business, the specific jobs vary greatly, perhaps more widely than jobs at the traditional banks do. In particular, given the volume of transactions that many of these organizations handle, there are excellent opportunities for people with strong technical skills.

Key Jobs for MBAs

The jobs available at different commercial banks vary significantly according to the scope of their operations. Mega-banks offer a huge variety of positions, from hard-core programming spots to investment banking and trading. Small and regional banks tend to have a narrower range of more traditional positions (loan officer, teller, credit analyst, and so on).

Sales. Here's relatively sure prospect for the uncertain future. Banks are competing with brokerages, investment banks, and mutual funds, all of which offer more obvious and alluring opportunities in sales. There is also a rising demand for salespeople who understand product development and investment managers (brokers). An undergraduate degree in finance, business, or economics gets you in the door. An MBA gets you a second interview.

Salary range: $30,000 to $100,000 or more (commissions and new business you bring in can add substantially to these figures).

Trust officer. Give this area a shot if you have a flair for financial counseling and if you like hobnobbing with high-net-worth individuals (folks with serious money). The job involves helping clients with trust services, estate planning, taxes, investing, and probate law. Warning: Sooner or later you'll find yourself in the middle of family squabbles, jealousies, disinheritances, and lawsuits. This job requires diplomacy, tact, deference, and a better, more current understanding of tax law than most attorneys need.

Salary range: $35,000 to $100,000.

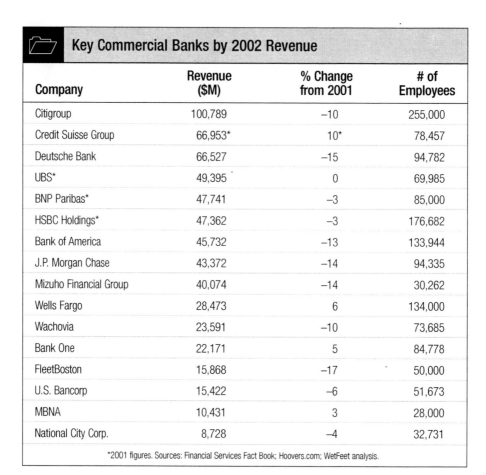

Key Commercial Banks by 2002 Revenue

Company	Revenue ($M)	% Change from 2001	# of Employees
Citigroup	100,789	−10	255,000
Credit Suisse Group	66,953*	10*	78,457
Deutsche Bank	66,527	−15	94,782
UBS*	49,395	0	69,985
BNP Paribas*	47,741	−3	85,000
HSBC Holdings*	47,362	−3	176,682
Bank of America	45,732	−13	133,944
J.P. Morgan Chase	43,372	−14	94,335
Mizuho Financial Group	40,074	−14	30,262
Wells Fargo	28,473	6	134,000
Wachovia	23,591	−10	73,685
Bank One	22,171	5	84,778
FleetBoston	15,868	−17	50,000
U.S. Bancorp	15,422	−6	51,673
MBNA	10,431	3	28,000
National City Corp.	8,728	−4	32,731

*2001 figures. Sources: Financial Services Fact Book; Hoovers.com; WetFeet analysis.

Additional Resources

American Banker Online (http://www.americanbanker.com/index.html)

American Bankers Association (http://www.aba.com/default.htm)

Hoover's Banks and Savings Institutions Industry Snapshot
(http://www.hoovers.com/industry/snapshot/profile/0,3519,7,00.html)

Knowledge @ Wharton: Finance and Investment
(http://knowledge.wharton.upenn.edu/category.cfm?catid=1)

McKinsey Quarterly: Financial Services
(http://www.mckinseyquarterly.com/category_editor.asp?L2=10)

Ohio State University List of Finance Sites
(http://www.cob.ohio-state.edu/fin/journal/jofsites.htm)

Computer Hardware

Industry Overview

Raise your hand if you still use a typewriter. Didn't think so. Despite the occasional slump in computer sales, computers are here to stay.

Computer hardware, as we use the term, means central processing units (CPUs), including memory and storage—in other words, the machine on which you run an operating system and application software and to which you attach peripherals.

Computer hardware and software are useless without each other. But working together they store, modify, and exchange data: words, pictures, and numbers—everything from correspondence to news photos, from drawings of jet aircraft to shipping manifests, from news releases to financial reports, from census statistics to stock quotes, from maps to e-mail.

The competition among PC makers, especially desktop PC makers, has become increasingly intense in the last few years, as once-premium devices have become commodity products, with little to differentiate them and razor-thin margins. HP's purchase of Compaq, which resulted in little change in the two companies' product lines, is an example of the former. And the falling revenues endemic to the industry speaks to the latter. Not to mention that, according to IDC, worldwide PC shipments were down 0.5 percent for the second quarter of 2002 compared to the same period in 2001, making for five consecutive quarterly declines. As a result, there's been continual downsizing in the computer hardware industry, with the survivors expected to take up the slack.

There are definite geographic concentrations in the hardware industry despite its worldwide reach. It's often noted that high-tech companies often locate near colleges and universities, and there's a good deal of truth to that, as many companies come out of research done at such institutions. Silicon Valley is near San Jose State, the University of California at Berkeley and Stanford University. Route 128 is near the educational Mecca of Cambridge, Massachusetts. Research Triangle in North Carolina and the area around Austin, Texas, are also good examples. Still, there are other places within North America where you'll find major companies: Gateway in North Dakota, Micron in Idaho, Corel in Ottawa and so on.

And most major corporations in these industries reach across national borders. International sales normally account for a large percentage of most hardware companies' bottom line and India, Japan, China, and Ireland are hotbeds of hardware manufacturing.

Trends

Consolidation. The boom of the '90s, with stock prices soaring, gave many large corporations the capital to purchase wholesale smaller (or sometimes, larger) companies—even, sometimes, competing companies. For example, Compaq bought Digital Equipment Corp., and shortly after, HP bought Compaq. During the digestion process, key technologies get killed off, divisions get axed, and often so-called synergies don't work out. The result is fewer employment opportunities (unless you're a merger manager).

Downsizing. Another effect of consolidations is downsizing. When larger companies merge, the job losses can reach five figures. But it's not just mergers and acquisitions that have caused layoffs: Busting dot coms that found they couldn't sell manicures over the Internet, consumers still scared of or just not buying, gluts of identical products, a limping economy—all contribute to net losses of jobs in many of the high-tech sectors.

Outsourcing. In the hardware world, increasingly more manufacturers are outsourcing products and components from overseas. Some companies are only doing design in the United States, leaving production to cheaper facilities in the Philippines, China, and elsewhere. What this means is that product managers and project heads may have to travel a lot more than in previous generations; it also means that many North America based jobs are being lost.

How It Breaks Down

For job seekers, one way to segment the industry is by the type of computer hardware the company makes. Other differentiating factors include industry and application focus and sales-and-distribution methodology: mail order, Internet, or retail.

Workstations (desktop and laptop). This is perhaps the most publicly visible segment of the high-tech hardware market, with computers becoming more and more common at work, home, labs, and educational institutions. There are cheap, nearly disposable models from eMachines and Packard-Bell; powerful home/SOHO desktops from established players such as Dell, Gateway, and Apple; and powerful, specialized workstations from Sun, SGI, and others used in 3D rendering, molecular modeling, computer-aided design (CAD), and video editing. Portable computers represent a growing overall share of the personal computer market, especially as laptops achieve near-parity performance with desktops (though at a higher price). Personal digital assistants (PDAs), though not as hot as they were with the general public a few years ago, are becoming more installed in professional milieus, being used to monitor warehouses, track shipments, and the like.

Overall, the market for all of the above has been grim, with the Goldman Sachs Hardware Index seeing lows in 2002 not experienced since 1998. After the dot-com bust, the demand for computers of all flavors, from servers to

PDAs, evaporated as downsizing companies across the world found too much hardware on their hands and consumers were reluctant to buy or upgrade. As a result, computer company after computer company has revised earning estimates downwards for the remainder of 2002.

Peripherals. A peripheral is usually understood to be an external product added to a computer, such as a new mouse, speakers, CD-RW burners and the like (check Kensington, Logitech, Keytronic, and others), all the way up to monitors, scanners, and printers. However, a peripheral can also be something added into a computer, such as a 3-D video card or an internal modem.

The difficulties of the market situation have caused some smaller manufacturers to close shop and some of the larger forces in the field, such as Epson, Xerox, and Canon (all make scanners, printers, and more), have also felt pinched. However, some segments such as the video card market (dominated by Nvidia, ATI, and Diamond) remain healthy.

Servers. There are many types of servers—those big boxes that, among other things, are the glue that holds the Internet together. In addition to Web servers, which pass back and forth all of the HTML and image files that end up on your screen, there are local area network (LAN) servers, wide area network (WAN), file servers, mail servers, database servers, and more. Every time two computers (termed in this context as "clients") connect over a network, a server is involved.

As a result, servers play a critical role in business, entertainment, and education—and as a result of that, entire industries have sprung up to ensure that individual server products, both hardware and software, are bulletproof. Companies such as IBM, Dell, HP, and others offer "big iron" hardware and often accompany product sales with service contracts of engineering teams to install and maintain the servers. Some companies such as Oracle sell specialized

hardware/software installations for databases; SAP does similar setups for companies needing to manage production and inventory. Ironically, it was this essential role that indirectly led to the downturn in the server market of the last few years. As the economy boomed, companies bought more equipment than they needed, anticipating an increase in bandwidth that never materialized. When demand fizzled and companies went bankrupt, there was a glut of server hardware and professional server administrators.

Key Jobs for MBAs

The job outlook for computer manufacturers—as for the high-tech industry in general—is currently quite weak. Still, while people with technical backgrounds will have an easier time with their job search, people without technical degrees can also find work.

Product manager. As a product manager, you're a key player in coming up with product ideas and working with engineers to make them a reality. This position requires some grasp of technical matters, the ability to build consensus and teamwork, and a knack for spotting—and anticipating—market trends. Most of these jobs require an MBA or comparable experience.

Salary range: $50,000 to $150,000.

Financial analyst. Financial analysis in computer hardware companies can take many forms: numerical analysis for production planning, industrial operations management, or general finance and accounting. In some cases, an analyst evaluates other companies as potential merger or acquisition targets. Depending on how the analyst position is defined, an MBA may be necessary.

Salary range: $60,000 to $80,000.

Key U.S. Computer Hardware Manufacturers by 2002 Revenue

Company	Revenue ($M)	% Change from 2001	# of Employees
IBM	81,186	−6	355,421
HP	56,588	25	141,000
Dell Computer Corp.	31,168	−2	34,600
Cisco Systems	18,915	−15	36,000
Xerox	15,849	−7	67,800
Sun Microsystems	12,496	−32	39,400
Seagate Technology	6,087	2	n/a
Apple Computer	5,742	7	10,211
EMC Corp.	5,438	−23	17,400
NCR	5,585	−6	29,700
Pitney Bowes	4,410	7	33,130
Gateway	4,171	−31	11,500
MicronPC	810	−19	1,000

Sources: Hoovers.com; WetFeet analysis.

Additional Resources

Association for Computer Machinery (http://www.acm.org)

ComputerWorld (http://www.computerworld.com)

Hoover's Computer Hardware Industry Snapshot
(http://www.hoovers.com/industry/snapshot/profile/0,3519,12,00.html)

Internet.com (http://www.internet.com/home-d.html)

McKinsey Quarterly: Computers and Technology
(http://www.mckinseyquarterly.com/category_editor.asp?L2=4)

Computer Software

Overview

Computer software products accomplish discrete tasks and are sold as complete packages. Computer software is distinct from enterprise software, which is usually sold as part of a large (and expensive) system integration/consulting project to automate entire business processes. Some computer software products are so-called applications, such as word processing and Web browsing. Com-puter software also includes operating systems, such as Windows, and utilities.

Businesses and individual consumers are the main purchasers of computer software, which is sold through both retail and business-to-business channels. In either case, companies that sell computer software are intensely focused on the needs and desires of customers. Probably the quickest way to talk yourself out of a job in this segment is to make the technology seem more important than the end user.

Marketing is critical to the success of any computer software product, partly because there are so many companies competing in the software market and partly because computers are still new to a lot of people. In fact, in most companies that produce computer software, the marketing department calls the shots.

At the other end of the totem pole, technical writers are employed at most computer software companies to write user documentation, either for publication in the form of manuals or, increasingly, as online help. The industry

also employs—in descending order of technical expertise—software testers, customer service reps, sales personnel, and staff for the usual coterie of business functions, from HR to accounting.

Trends

More powerful software. Faster computers, as well as the fact that many PCs now come with fancy video cards, have made it possible for software developers to go to market with exciting, new products. For instance, computer-design software now allows designers to develop ideas in 3-D, rather than just two dimensions. Companies like Autodesk, Dassault, EDS, and PTC are trying to capitalize on the market for 3-D design tools. And computer games get more realistic—or fantastic, depending on how you look at it—every year.

The Internet. The Internet has meant a sea change in the software industry. Many software users now download their purchases from software providers' websites, forgoing diskettes and packaging and getting straight to business. And the subscription ASP (application service provider) model, in which users access software and databases that are stored on the vendors' servers via the Web, is proving attractive for makers of all kinds of products in areas from gaming to business software. One projection states that in 2005, 67 percent of all software sales will be via the Internet, compared to 12 percent in 2001.

Linux. Linux system software, the centerpiece of the open-source movement (which champions free software for all, and welcomes and encourages developer contributions to the free software), is finally making a splash in the business world. More companies, like Credit Suisse First Boston and Merrill Lynch, are seeing the benefits of not having to pay for software and upgrades and beginning to adopt Linux environments. Computer makers like Dell and HP are shipping PCs loaded with Linux. And big business-software providers like BEA, SAP, and Veritas are making products that run on Linux.

Copyright-protection battles. The entertainment industry is currently trying to get the government to require that PCs, handheld computers, and other devices used to play or record entertainment products (MP3s, DVD movies, etc.) must come with embedded copyright-protection software. This would allow the entertainment industry to protect its copyrighted products from piracy. It would also mean that Linux is illegal, peer-to-peer file-sharing systems would all but dry up and blow away, and most likely the additional cost of the copyright-protection software would be passed on to consumers. Open-source advocates point to the VCR market—which the motion-picture industry similarly tried to stifle back in the 1980s, and which now provides movie studios with 46 percent of their revenue—as proof that the market will reward the entertainment industry without embedded copyright-protection laws.

Tough times for business software. For the first time in ten years, software sales to major and mid-sized business customers declined, by 1 percent (to $78.9 billion) in 2001. A big portion of that decline was due to the miserable showing by Internet-commerce software providers, including formerly red-hot companies like CommerceOne and Ariba, which saw sales decline by more than 30 percent.

How It Breaks Down

The computer software market is most commonly segmented according to the type of work a product does. A few of the major market segments are listed below, along with the names of a few companies that are active in each.

System software. Microsoft's Windows is by far the dominant example in his category-but not the only one. Apple's MacOS is still alive and well, and Unix, including Linux, is a force in the server market. HP, Sun Microsystems, IBM, and Silicon Graphics provide versions of Unix with servers they manufacture. Red Hat has actually made a business out of selling a version of Linux, which is also available free on the Internet.

Productivity. Personal productivity includes word processing, spreadsheets, presentations, database management, graphic design, and other applications that help people do their jobs. Key players: Adobe (PageMaker, PhotoShop, Illustrator), Microsoft (Word, PowerPoint, Excel).

Education. Educational software helps your kids learn to read, teaches you about geography or a foreign language, stimulates logical thinking, and so on. This category also comprises children's educational games, the nascent electronic-book industry, teaching resources, and music instruction. Key players: Cendant Corporation and Disney.

Finance. Financial software includes applications for small business and personal accounting, personal finance, and tax preparation. Key players: Intuit (maker of Quicken), Block Financial (the Kiplinger titles), Microsoft.

Internet. Internet software includes more than the two leading browsers, which are produced by Netscape and Microsoft. Sun Microsystems and some other companies dream of breaking Microsoft's dominance by developing software that you don't buy. Instead, you rent it as needed, downloading it via the Internet. This category also includes software for creating websites, from companies like Macromedia.

Utilities. Utilities help you keep your computer running by diagnosing and fixing problems. Symantec (Norton Utilities) is a leading developer.

Games. A highly competitive and extremely broad market segment, this includes role-playing software, auto and flight simulation, sports, strategy games such as chess, and children's games. Key players: Electronic Arts, GT Interactive, Hasbro Interactive, Broderbund. Also, note that there are many small, thriving studios that use the bigger players for distribution and marketing, as well as big-name individual designers—Sid Meyer, Ron Martinez, Will Wright, Jim Gasperini—who will work for game companies on a project-by-project basis.

Reference. Homes, schools, and businesses are getting rid of old bound reference collections in favor of CD-ROM reference tools that offer portability, lightning-fast searches, and interactive media. This market segment includes encyclopedias, dictionaries, atlases, Internet guides, and zip code directories. Key players: Microsoft, Grolier Interactive.

Key Job for MBAs

Product or project manager. Product managers take the software title from conception through development to the finished product. You define the features that the product will encompass and work with teams of designers, engineers, writers, and quality-assurance testers. Product managers typically hold MBAs or have extensive experience in the software field.

Salary range: $55,000 to $90,000, with more-senior product managers (with three to five years' experience) making $70,000 to $110,000.

Key Computer Software Companies by 2002 Revenue

Company	Revenue ($M)	% Change from 2001	# of Employees
IBM	81,186	−6	355,421
Microsoft	28,365	12	50,500
Oracle	9,675	−11	42,006
SAP	7,786	19	28,878
Computer Associates	2,964	−29	16,600
Sungard Data Systems	2,530	31	8,800
PeopleSoft	1,949	−6	8,293
Compuware	1,729	−14	10,164
Siebel Systems	1,635	−20	5,909
Veritas Software	1,507	1	5,647
Cadence Design Systems	1,293	−10	5,175
BMC Software	1,289	−14	6,335
MicronPC	810	−19	1,000

Sources: Hoovers.com; WetFeet analysis.

Additional Resources

ComputerWorld (http://www.computerworld.com)

Developer.com (http://www.developer.com)

Hoover's Computer Software Industry Snapshot
(http://www.hoovers.com/industry/snapshot/profile/0,3519,13,00.html)

Internet.com (http://www.internet.com/home-d.html)

McKinsey Quarterly: Computers and Technology
(http://www.mckinseyquarterly.com/category_editor.asp?L2=4)

Consulting

Industry Overview

So, you want to be a consultant? Or, more likely, you think you'll spend a few years as one and then move on to other things. You're not alone—there are more than 250,000 consultants in the United States. Consulting firms are traditionally among the largest employers of top MBA and college graduates, and they are an attractive alternative career option for people who've toiled in industry for a number of years.

Consulting is a high-paying, high-profile field that offers you the opportunity to take on a large degree of responsibility right out of school and quickly learn a great deal about the business world. It's also a profession that will send you to the far corners of the country—and leave you there for days and weeks on end while you sort out tough questions for a client that's paying your firm millions of dollars.

In essence, consultants are hired advisors to corporations. They tackle a wide variety of business problems and provide solutions for their clients. Depending on the size and chosen strategy of the firm, these problems can be as straightforward as researching a new market, as technically challenging as designing and coding a large manufacturing control system, as sensitive as providing outplacement services for the HR department, or as sophisticated as totally rethinking the client's organization and strategy.

Management consultants must be skilled at conducting research and analyzing it. Research means collecting raw data from a variety of sources including the client's computers, trade associations in the client's industry, government agencies, and, perhaps most importantly, surveys and market studies that you devise and implement yourself. It also means interviewing people to gather anecdotal information and expert opinion. The interviewees may be anyone, from industry experts to the client's top executives to the client's lowest-level employees. All this data must then be analyzed, using tools from spreadsheets to your own brain. The idea here is to spot behavior patterns, production bottlenecks, market movements, and other trends and conditions that affect a client's business.

Your ultimate job is to improve the client's business by effecting changes in response to your analysis. That's the hard part, because it involves convincing the client to accept your recommendations, often in the face of opposition from client executives who resent outsiders upstaging them with the boss or resistance from company employees who have something to lose from change. To succeed you'll need excellent people skills and the ability to put together a persuasive PowerPoint presentation. Finally, you'll need the ability to handle disappointment if your solution fails or the client decides not to even try implementing it.

One good thing about the advice business: Companies always seem to want more. As evidence, the consulting industry has been on a sustained growth binge for well more than a decade. One other thing about the consulting business: The product really is the people, and firms compete on the basis of who's the smartest and the hardest working. As a result, each firm wants to hire the best and the brightest. If you're one of them—you probably know if you are—you'll have a good shot at landing one of these competitive jobs.

Trends

Bad times in consulting. The weak economy and the falling stock market, as well as the terrorist attacks of September 11, 2001, combined to hit Corporate America hard. In response, corporations got ruthless about cutting nonessential costs. Guess what's high on the list of nonessential costs for many companies? Right: consulting engagements. In addition, with companies spending less on IT systems, the industry no longer makes out like a bandit on implementation projects like it did in the 1990s; demand for IT consulting fell by 6 percent in 2001. As a result, layoffs have hit just about every consulting firm you can think of, large numbers of smaller concerns have gone under, and those who have managed to keep their jobs often no longer enjoy the kinds of perks they enjoyed just a few years back.

The end of e-consulting? A couple of years ago, e-business boutique firms such as marchFIRST (now out of business) were on top of the consulting game. Clients needed to go digital, and industry giants like Deloitte Consulting scrambled to keep up with novice Internet firms and their 30-year-old CEOs. But in today's environment, the e-consulting business has lost substantial steam. The question is, will it survive at all?

Some signs look pretty grim. Internet consulting firms lost the bulk of their clientele to the dot-com decline, and firms across the industry have suffered through substantial layoffs and plummeting stock prices—that is, if they've managed to stay in business at all.

For most consulting firms, e-consulting opportunities still exist, but they've greatly declined. With less funding and a tougher economy, many surviving Internet start-ups can't afford to purchase consulting services. And old-economy companies looking at expanding their Web presence are warier than they might have been a couple of years ago about laying out wads of cash to consulting firms to do so. All this spells hard times for e-consultants.

Recruiting drought. It's another down year for consulting recruiting. Many consulting firms don't have enough business to keep their existing staff busy, so, in addition to laying off employees, they're cutting back on the number of new recruits they're looking to bring onboard. Look for consulting firms to have considerably fewer offers to make on campus this year—and look for some firms that have recruited on campus in the past to skip your school altogether.

Consulting, or outsourcing? When is someone who's called a consultant and employed by a consulting firm not actually a consultant? Traditionally, consulting firms offered client companies business advice. In the 1990s, many firms moved away from advice and towards system implementation—in which, in addition to advice, the consultants helped install new systems and integrate them with clients' existing systems. Now consulting firms are moving even further away from the traditional definition by relying increasingly on outsourcing for revenues. This model sees consulting firms taking on specific business functions like IT and HR for client companies. Firms like Accenture, Cap Gemini Ernst & Young, and IBM (which acquired PwC Consulting in 2002) are seeing major growth in these offerings.

How It Breaks Down

Even though there are thousands of consulting organizations across the country, these firms can be tough to get a handle on. Why? Most are privately held, work directly with other businesses rather than with your average consumer, and tend to be intensely private about the names of the clients they work with and the actual work they do. Nevertheless, if you want to get a job in the industry, you're going to have to know which firms do what and be able to say in clear and convincing terms why French vanilla is oh-so-much-better than vanilla with little specks of vanilla bean sprinkled throughout.

To help you understand the consulting landscape, we've divided the industry into six different categories: the industry elite, the Big Five, boutiques, information technology (IT) consultancies, human resources specialists, and the independents. Most players in the industry can be put into one or more of these different categories.

Industry elite. The rich and famous of the consulting world. These companies focus on providing cutting-edge strategy and operations advice to the top management of large corporations. They generally hire the best candidates from the best undergraduate, MBA, and other graduate programs. Slackers need not apply. Players in this group include: A.T. Kearney, Bain & Co., Booz Allen Hamilton, the Boston Consulting Group, McKinsey & Co., Mercer, and Monitor Group, to name a few.

Big Five. These were the consulting operations of the Big Five accounting firms, all of which—except for Deloitte Consulting—were spun off and/or sold over the past couple of years. Although these firms provide some of the same strategy and operations advice as the elite, they tend to put a stronger emphasis on implementation work, particularly in the IT world. The players are Accenture, Deloitte Consulting, Cap Gemini Ernst & Young, BearingPoint (formerly KPMG Consulting), and IBM Business Consulting Services (formerly PricewaterhouseCoopers Consulting). (And, until recently, [Arthur] Andersen.) Four of the Big Five (now referred to as the Big Four with the demise of Andersen) got out of the consulting business, partly because of SEC concerns over possible conflicts of interest, which have led to overly rosy audits of firms that are consulting clients of the accounting firm performing the audit. This was an issue in Andersen's dealings with Enron.

Boutique. Firms that specialize along industry or functional lines. Although often smaller, these firms may have top reputations and do the same operations and strategy work the elite firms do, but with more of an industry focus.

Representative players include: Advisory Board Company and APM (health care); Corporate Executive Board (cross-company research); Marakon Associates (strategy), Oliver Wyman (financial services); MarketBridge, formerly Oxford Associates (sales); PRTM (high-tech operations); Strategic Decisions Group (decision analysis), Roland Berger Strategy Consultants (strategy and operations); Braun Consulting, formerly Vertex Partners (strategy).

IT. Although Internet consulting firms have suffered in the past year and a half, information technology specialists can still find jobs in the consulting world. The technology practices of the Big Five and Big Five-related firms (Accenture, Deloitte Consulting, Cap Gemini Ernst & Young, BearingPoint, and IBM Business Consulting Services) have slowed but not disappeared, and tech giants such as IBM have snatched up struggling e-consultancies (Mainspring in this case), not to mention one of the Big Five (PwC Consulting was gobbled up by IBM in 2002). IT consulting focuses on providing advice, implementation, and programming work on issues related to computer systems, telecommunications, and the Internet. Representative players include American Management Systems, Computer Sciences Corp., DiamondCluster, Electronic Data Systems Corporation, and the current and former Big Five–related firms.

Human resources. This area of consulting focuses on personnel issues such as employee management and evaluation systems, payroll and compensation programs, pensions, and other benefits programs. Representative firms include The Hay Group, Hewitt Associates, William M. Mercer, Sibson & Co., Towers Perrin, and Watson Wyatt & Company. In addition, several of the Big Five firms have practices devoted to this area.

Independents. One-man or one-woman shops. By sheer numbers, independent consultants far outnumber the larger firms-fully 45 percent of all consultants are reported to be independents. They typically have some sort of industry or functional specialty and get hired on a project basis. If you have an MBA and

several years of useful and topical business experience, there's no reason not to hang out a shingle yourself.

Key Jobs for MBAs

Associate/consultant/senior consultant. This is the typical port of entry for newly minted MBAs (and increasingly for non-MBA graduate students as well). Senior consultants often perform research and analysis, formulate recommendations, and present findings to the client. Oh, and at many firms, they have to implement those great ideas, too. Although this is usually a tenure-track position, a fair number of consultants will leave the business after two or three years to pursue entrepreneurial or industry positions.

Salary range: $65,000 to $130,000 or more with bonus.

Manager. After a few years, a senior consultant will move up to manager. As the title implies, this usually means leading a team of consultants and analysts toward project completion. Some firms may hire MBAs with significant work experience directly into the manager position, particularly in their IT practices. In addition to having more-rigorous responsibilities for managing the project team, the manager will typically be a primary point person for client interactions.

Salary range: $70,000 to $150,000.

Partner or VP. Congratulations! You've forded the River Jordan of consulting and arrived at the Promised Land. Note that some firms further subdivide partners into junior and senior grade. And, if you aspire to it, there's always that chairman or CEO position. As a partner, one of your big responsibilities will be to sell new work. Fortunately, as with other big-ticket sales jobs, the pay can be quite rewarding.

Salary range: $250,000 to several million dollars at leading firms.

Key Consulting Companies by 2002 Revenue

Company	Revenue ($M)	% Change from 2001	# of Employees
Electronic Data Systems	21,502	0	137,000
Accenture	13,105	0	75,000
Computer Sciences Corp.	11,426	9	67,000
Cap Gemini Ernst & Young	7,455	14	57,760
IBM Business Consulting Svcs	6,400	−14	30,000
McKinsey & Co.	3,300	−3	12,000
Deloitte Consulting	3,150	−10	12,000
Mercer	2,400	9	15,000
BearingPoint	2,368	−17	9,300
Booz Allen Hamilton	2,100	0	11,510
Hewitt Associates	1,750	18	14,600
Towers Perrin	1,400	−5	8,000
Boston Consulting Group	1,020	−3	4,000
American Management Systems	987	−17	6,300
Bain & Co.*	825	2	2,800
Watson Wyatt & Co.	711	2	4,250
A.T. Kearney	434	7	5,000
Navigant Consulting	258	10	1,368
Corporate Executive Board	162	27	997
DiamondCluster Int'l	203	−22	1,121
Charles River Associates	131	19	490
Advisory Board Co.	81	27	445

*2001 figures. Sources: Hoovers.com; WetFeet analysis.

WetFeet®

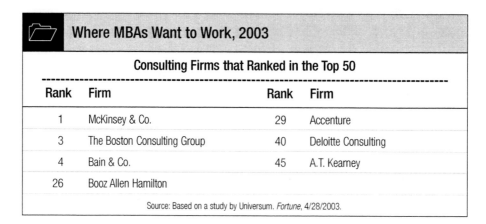

Where MBAs Want to Work, 2003

Consulting Firms that Ranked in the Top 50

Rank	Firm	Rank	Firm
1	McKinsey & Co.	29	Accenture
3	The Boston Consulting Group	40	Deloitte Consulting
4	Bain & Co.	45	A.T. Kearney
26	Booz Allen Hamilton		

Source: Based on a study by Universum. *Fortune*, 4/28/2003.

Additional Resources

ConsultingCentral.com (http://www.consultingcentral.com)

Fuqua School of Business Consulting Club
(http://www.duke.edu/web/fuquacc)

Hoover's Computer Services Industry Snapshot
(http://www.hoovers.com/industry/snapshot/profile/0,3519,58,00.html)

McKinsey Quarterly (http://www.mckinseyquarterly.com)

WetFeet®

Industries

Consumer Electronics

Industry Overview

Think about it: 98 percent of all U.S. households have a color television, 70 percent have a cordless phone, 52 percent a CD player, and 30 percent a camcorder. Now think about the engineers, designers, marketers, salespeople, customer service reps, and finance gurus who design, manufacture, and market all those PalmPilots, Game Boys, DiscMans, DVD players, StarTAC cell phones, and other electronic gadgets. The consumer electronics industry is big time.

Although much of the actual manufacturing is done in Asia and other low labor-cost locations, other functions have remained in the United States. On the technical side, opportunities exist for software and electronics engineers, as well as quality assurance engineers, industrial designers, manufacturing design engineers, and IT professionals. If you're a people person—if you can design a marketing campaign, close a distribution deal with a major retail chain, write marketing copy, or help a confused consumer understand a complex product—consumer electronics companies may be good places for you, too.

You can earn your stripes at a multinational corporation like Samsung or Mitsubishi, where big money is backing big products like high-definition television (HDTV) and smart phones (a combined wireless phone/PDA). Or you can try your hand at a young start-up that's pushing the consumer-electronics envelope in one market niche or another. So before you start your job search, think about whether you like the structure and resources (and bureaucracy) that a big organization will have or whether you prefer the flexibility and cutting-edge spirit (and bare-bones budget) of a new company.

Industries

Job seekers should also keep in mind that consumer electronics are global brands, so many companies have opportunities for international positions and travel, and foreign language skills are often highly desirable. (In fact, the three largest manufacturers are foreign-based—Sony and Matsushita in Japan, Philips in the Netherlands.) And in the United States, though there is some concentration of consumer electronics jobs on the East and West Coasts, the industry is sprawled across the country. Many of the large companies have multiple offices to choose from, with each location housing a different product line or corporate function.

Trends

More than just entertainment. As it has gone digital, the consumer electronics industry has evolved way beyond televisions and stereos. Many consumers are buying newly inexpensive computers to exchange e-mail and surf the Web. Pagers and cell phones—once purely for business use—have become indispensable for families on the go. But the bigger long-term change will come from the transformation of traditional consumer items to digital technology. DVDs are currently the biggest thing in the industry. Cameras, music recorders, and televisions are all going digital. November 1, 1999, saw the first digital television broadcasts, which may turn out to have been a turning point of momentous proportions (though mass acceptance of digital TV is still quite a way off). And digitization has made possible some brand-new electronic toys, such as consumer-priced global positioning systems. Consumer electronics products are insinuating themselves into the furthest recesses of our lives. Even our homes are being automated, and some new home construction includes wiring for digital appliances.

Intellectual property confusion. Since the first big digital consumer product, the audio CD, hit the market in the early 1980s, nothing has slowed the juggernaut,

with one exception: worries about pirating—of music and, more recently, of movies. Such concerns delayed the introduction of writable CD equipment (and digital audio tape), and the spread of the MP3 format for recording music and exchanging it via the Internet is giving the music industry conniptions. The spread of Internet-assisted piracy (Have you downloaded any copyrighted files lately? We thought so.) may be delaying industry growth while lawyers work out licensing arrangements and companies fight to force equipment makers to produce products that will help them protect their copyrights.

How It Breaks Down

The consumer electronics industry includes manufacturers of all shapes and sizes. The largest are multinational conglomerates with more than 100,000 employees and interests in many different industries. The smallest often have only one office with less than 50 employees focused on one product. In the middle are manufacturers that offer a range of products within a certain category, such as speakers and audio accessories. Because companies of all sizes can make similar products, industry observers usually break down the market by product category rather than company size.

Video. These days, all eyes are on video. As the switch is made from analog to digital technology, the market is quickly expanding beyond traditional televisions, VCRs, and camcorders to include digital televisions, digital versatile disc (DVD) players, home theater systems, home satellite systems, and set-top Internet access devices. Key players include Matsushita (Panasonic), Philips (Magnavox), Sony, Thompson (RCA), TiVo, and Microsoft (WebTV).

Audio. Vinyl may be the latest retro resurgence, but it can't stop the digital wave. Consumers can now choose from CDs, DVDs, MiniDiscs, and MP3s (a computer file format that lets you download music from the Internet) to get digital-quality sound. The proliferation of digital formats is also driving new

demand for upgraded home theater systems, multimedia PCs, car stereos, and portable players. Key players include Bose (speakers), Harman International, Sony (MiniDisc), and Toshiba (DVD).

Mobile and wireless. Mobile electronics and wireless technology have transformed communication. Better technology and lower prices have turned high-end products like cell phones and pagers into commodities sold out of street-side kiosks. And broad market demand is fueling the race to develop the next generation of phones, pagers, and PDAs, which will use digital cellular, digital personal communication service (PCS), and wireless modems to interconnect. High-end car audio, security, navigation, and multimedia systems manufacturers are also taking advantage of the new digital technologies and making inroads in the mass market. Key players include 3Com (PalmPilot), Motorola, Nokia, Philips, and Clarion (AutoPC).

Multimedia. Multimedia products create an interactive experience for the user by combining sound, graphics, text, and video. The personal computer is the main delivery platform for multimedia products, although the digital television will also offer a multimedia experience. Again, digital is the word to watch. For PC users, DVD-ROMs offer better speed and storage capabilities than CD-ROMs. Digital cameras save digitized images in a memory cache, rather than on film. Software plug-ins, which can be downloaded from the Internet, let users experience streaming audio and video applications on their PCs. And new video game consoles let players interact while playing games that include robust graphics and sound. Key players include Canon, Creative Technology (Sound Blaster), Nintendo (Game Boy, GameCube), Sony (PlayStation), Microsoft (Xbox), and Toshiba (DVD-ROM).

Integrated home systems. Picture this: While sitting at your computer at work, you pull up the website for your home, check out the live video feed to make sure your new puppy isn't devouring the muffins you forgot to put back in the cupboard this morning, click a link to preheat the oven for dinner, and turn up the thermostat to warm the house. This is the smart home. Smart homes are powered by integrated home systems—electronic products that are networked together and connected to the rest of the world via the Internet or wireless technology. Players in this fledgling market include IBM (Home Director), and appliance manufacturers like Sunbeam and Whirlpool are joining the fray by experimenting with products that are networkable.

Key Jobs for MBAs

Inventing, designing, building, manufacturing, distributing, and selling consumer electronics is a big business that requires lots of people with lots of different skills. On the business side, this industry employs marketers, customer service professionals, and operations specialists.

Marketer. Marketers are the people who convince consumers to buy consumer electronics products that, let's face it, in most cases they don't really need. Responsibilities can include pricing strategy, distribution, promotion, advertising, and public relations. Marketers analyze market trends, prepare sales forecasts, and manage inventory levels. Some also coordinate trade show preparation. Entry-level positions often require a bachelor's degree in business or marketing, while product-management positions usually require an MBA. Candidates should have strong analytical, business-planning, and presentation skills, plus good creative judgment.

Salary range: $35,000 to $200,000.

Key Consumer Electronics Companies by 2002 Revenue

Company	Revenue ($M)	% Change from 2001	# of Employees
General Electric Co.	130,685	4	315,000
Sony	62,280	9	168,000
Hitachi	60,104	−12	306,989
Matsushita Electric Ind.	51,830	−15	297,196
Philips Electronics	33,421	16	170,087
Samsung Electronics	24,463	−10	n/a
LG Electronics	18,602	48	51,300
Sanyo Electric Co.	15,881	−12	80,500
Emerson Electric	13,824	−11	111,500
Whirlpool Corp.	11,016	7	68,000
Thomson Corp.	7,756	7	42,000
Pioneer Corp.	5,029	−1	31,220
Kenwood Corp.	2,281	−5	8,820
Daewoo Electronics	2,290	−9	5,110
Harman Int'l Industries	1,826	6	10,389
Aiwa Co.	1,480	−36	4,739

Sources: Hoovers.com; WetFeet analysis.

Additional Resources

Consumer Electronics Association (http://www.ce.org)

Electronics Industries Alliance (http://www.eia.org)

Electronics Technicians Association, International
(http://www.eta-sda.com)

Consumer Products

Industry Overview

Consumer products is one of those elastic phrases that can include any of the jars, boxes, cans, or tubes on your kitchen and bathroom shelves—or it can expand to include pretty much everything you charged on your Visa card last year. This industry manufactures and, perhaps more important, markets everything from food and beverages to toiletries and small appliances. (We do not include industries sometimes put in this category but covered in other profiles: autos, apparel, entertainment products, and consumer durables, which are large appliances and other products expected to last more than three years).

The consumer products industry can be divided into four groups: beverages, food, toiletries and cosmetics, and small appliances. Most firms offer products that fit primarily into only one of these groups, although a firm may have a smattering of brands that cross the lines. Virtually all companies are similar in organizational structure, emphasis on brand management, and approach to business.

Consumer products are the foundation of the modern, consumer economy. The industry itself not only generates an enormous portion of the gross domestic product, it also pumps huge amounts of money into other industries, notably advertising and retail. Individual consumers make up the majority of this industry's customers; sales are concentrated in the United States, Japan, and Western Europe, though other parts of the world are working hard for the privileges of wearing clothing emblazoned with company logos, eating processed food, and chopping vegetables with an electric motor instead of a

traditional utensil. Success in consumer products is all about marketing an individual product, often by promoting a brand name. The competition is ferocious for shelf space, so package design, marketing, and customer satisfaction are key elements.

The majority of companies that sell consumer packaged goods are conglomerates consisting of many diverse subsidiaries selling brands that consumers recognize. Nabisco sells Milk-Bone pet snacks and Chips Ahoy! Cookies. Sara Lee Corporation produces products from Ball Park franks and Pickwick tea to Hanes underwear and Endust furniture polish. Unilever, an industry giant based in England, sells teas and soups, pasta and pizza sauces, ice cream, bath soaps, shampoo, salad dressing, margarine, laundry detergent, toothpaste, cosmetics, frozen foods, and perfumes. Clorox makes bleach, charcoal, Combat roach killer, and Hidden Valley salad dressing. Other big players in the industry include Keebler Foods and Nestle.

Trends

Size matters. A spate of mergers and acquisitions in recent years has resulted in a smaller group of larger giants—this is not an industry with a lot of boutique enterprises and garage entrepreneurs. (Recent industry acquisitions include PepsiCo's purchase of Quaker Oats, Kraft's purchase of Nabisco, and General Mills's purchase of Pillsbury.) There's no doubt about it: The conglomerates hold the power positions in this industry. Size gives them economies of scale, and a diversity of products gives them protection against down cycles. Which is not to say that cute little mail-order pickle-and-jam companies don't crop up every now and then and make a serious go of it. They do. These places aren't where the majority of the jobs are, however—at least not until Unilever or Nestle takes them over.

Name brands and global brands. Branding has become the religion of consumer marketing. Positive associations with a brand name make the difference between hot-selling products and stay-on-the-shelf losers. To increase margins, companies are investing in brands with worldwide appeal and eliminating those of marginal value. Unilever, for example, announced in late 1999 that it would eliminate more than 1,000 of its 1,600 or so brands, putting most of its resources behind about 400 so-called power brands, which are recognized internationally. And discount retailers are building more lucrative businesses by becoming exclusive providers of product lines with recognizable brand names; for instance, Kmart has Martha Stewart, and Target has Mossimo.

Private-label and store brands. Meanwhile, many full-price retailers are introducing private-label brands (a.k.a. store brands), with a goal of pumping up sales by offering products for less than they'd cost if premium-branded. The concept is simple: Put the store's label on a less-expensive alternative to the national brand. The product is the same, or close to the same; the brand name, and usually the price, is not. This trend has become particularly noticeable in the grocery business, where stores have invested in major advertising campaigns to build consumer confidence in their products. It's also noticeable in apparel; for instance, private-label products accounted for 16 percent of Federated's department-store revenue in 2001.

Overseas production. In its hunger for better margins, Levi's has moved nearly all of its manufacturing overseas. Despite the PR risks involved (just ask Nike), the lower costs resulting from cheap labor and less-stringent environmental regulations are increasingly causing profit-hungry consumer-products companies to consider overseas production facilities.

How It Breaks Down

Beverages. Intensely competitive and hugely reliant on advertising, this is a mature industry. Different segments of the beverage world include beer (Adolph Coors, Anheuser-Busch, Phillip Morris, Miller, Stroh's), soft drinks (Coca-Cola, PepsiCo, Cadbury Schweppes, National Beverage), and juices (Minute Maid by Coca-Cola).

Foods. There may be a little less consolidation in the food industry than in beverages, but this is also a mature and competitive industry with single-digit growth. Most of the packaged goods that fill our pantries, cupboards, and refrigerators come from a handful of big-league corporate players. Some are household names; Campbell Soup, Dole, General Mills, H.J. Heinz, and Kellogg have spent enormous sums of money to tattoo their names onto your brain. Other big players, such as Kraft and ConAgra (Hunt's, Healthy Choice, and Wesson) are better known for brands they own.

Toiletries, cosmetics, and cleaning products. Baby boomers aren't getting any younger, and vanity will outlast us all. So will household dirt. So this is a solid category for the foreseeable future. At three-and-one-half times the size of its nearest competitor, Procter & Gamble is the Godzilla of this group—and indeed the consumer products world in general. Other players include Avon Products, Clorox, Colgate-Palmolive, Revlon, Gillette, Kimberly-Clark (Huggies, Kotex, and Kleenex), Unilever, Johnson & Johnson, and SC Johnson (Pledge, Glade, Windex, Raid, OFF!, Edge, Ziploc, Shout, and Drano).

Small appliances. This is an amalgam of companies in various industries. More people are building and buying homes, and forecasters don't expect the trend to slow. So tools, kitchen gadgets, air-conditioners, chain saws, and anything else Saturday shoppers enjoy pausing over in the hardware store are selling well, and the future looks rosy for this segment of the industry. Nevertheless, this is also

a relatively mature industry, and the brand system is not as strong as it is in the other categories mentioned above. Players here include Black & Decker, Sunbeam, Sears, and Snap-On.

Key Jobs for MBAs

This is a hierarchical business and though merit and hard work count for a lot, even the wunderkinds have to do time before they're promoted. Senior management positions in marketing, operations, R&D, and other departments tend to be filled from within the company (or at least, from within the industry).

Marketing assistant or analyst. If you've just graduated from college, these are the trenches which prepare you for product management and brand management. Some of the work here is administrative, but your ideas are welcome and the brand management team will depend on your organizational ability as much as your knowledge of the target customer. An MBA will typically start as an assistant brand manager for a few years before being put in charge of shepherding all the product pieces to market. In either case, you can expect a lot of poring over sales and merchandising figures, Nielsen ratings, and premiums. Compensation varies widely depending on the company and its location, as well as where you went to school and your relevant experience.

Salary range: $25,000 to $70,000.

Product or brand manager. Conjure up your gloomiest images of what shopping was like in the Soviet Union. This is the fate product managers work to save us from. They create the catchy new names and novel packaging. They ask prospective customers how to make products even more irresistible. Then they scramble like mad for prominent display space, ad dollars, and their marketing director's active support. You either work your way up the ladder to

these jobs or start at this rung with an MBA. Very important reminder: Headhunters really love successful product managers.

Salary range: $45,000 to $100,000 or more.

Market researcher. To do this job, you don't really have to wear glasses and ask silly questions—you do have to have a strong interest in the psychology of customer behavior and an ability to coax this information out of prospective purchasers. Tools of the trade include focus groups, one-on-one interviews, Nielsen data, and quantitative surveys. People can enter these positions from undergraduate, MBA, or industry backgrounds.

Salary range: $30,000 to $100,000.

Manufacturing or finance manager. Because of the just-in-time inventory pressures, manufacturing and production plants also increasingly need MBAs with creative financing skills to help solve problems, assess profitability, and acquire new businesses. In some companies, these finance analysts and managers actually have equal and occasionally even greater authority than marketers. They aren't responsible for the presentations to senior management or the coordination with advertising, but they make many of the important recommendations and decisions that direct the course of new product development.

Salary range: $50,000 to $60,000 and up.

Key Consumer Products Companies by 2002 Revenue

Company	Revenue ($M)	% Change from 2001	# of Employees
Nestle	64,258	27	254,199
Unilever	50,698	10	247,000
Proctor & Gamble	40,238	3	102,000
Johnson & Johnson	36,298	10	108,300
Kraft Foods	29,723	−12	109,000
Philip Morris Int'l	28,672	8	40,000
ConAgra	27,630	2	89,000
PepsiCo	25,112	−7	142,000
Tyson Foods	23,367	117	120,000
Coca-Cola Co.	19,564	−3	56,000
Sara Lee Corp.	17,628	−1	154,900
L'oreal	14,975	23	50,491
Groupe Danone	14,237	10	92,209
Kimberly-Clark	13,566	−7	63,900
Anheuser-Busch	13,566	5	23,176
H.J. Heinz Co.	9,431	0	46,500
Colgate-Palmolive Co.	9,294	−1	37,700
Cadbury Schweppes	8,538	6	42,848
Gillette Co.	8,453	−6	30,300
Kellogg Co.	8,304	−6	25,700
Newell Rubbermaid	7,454	8	47,000

Sources: Hoovers.com; WetFeet analysis.

Industries

Additional Resources

BrandWeek (http://www.brandweek.com/brandweek/index.jsp)

Hoover's Apparel, Shoes, and Accessories Industry Snapshot
(http://www.hoovers.com/industry/snapshot/profile/0,3519,42,00.html)

Hoover's Beverages Industry Snapshot
(http://www.hoovers.com/industry/snapshot/profile/0,3519,8,00.html)

Hoover's Food Industry Snapshot
http://www.hoovers.com/industry/snapshot/profile/0,3519,19,00.html)

Hoover's Personal Care & Household Cleaning Products Industry Snapshot
http://www.hoovers.com/industry/snapshot/profile/0,3519,24,00.html)

Hoover's Sporting Goods Industry Snapshot
http://www.hoovers.com/industry/snapshot/profile/0,3519,55,00.html)

Hoover's Toys & Games Industry Snapshot
(http://www.hoovers.com/industry/snapshot/profile/0,3519,44,00.html)

Knowledge @ Wharton: Marketing
(http://knowledge.wharton.upenn.edu/category.cfm?catid=4)

MarketingPower.com (http://www.marketingpower.com)

McKinsey Quarterly: Marketing
(http://www.mckinseyquarterly.com/category_editor.asp?L2=16)

ProductScan Online (http://www.productscan.com/)

Energy & Utilities

Industry Overview

The industrial revolution started with the steam engine and is still dependent on energy produced from natural resources. The process begins when energy companies extract fossil fuels such as oil, coal, and natural gas from Mother Earth. These natural resources are turned into electricity and delivered to the consumer's door by power utilities companies, or they are processed into fuels, such as gasoline, propane, heating oil, or industrial coke for making steel. They are supplemented by water-powered hydroelectric generators and by uranium-powered nuclear generators. In any case, the result is the energy on which industrial countries are dependent. Without it we could not run our home appliances or our factories, travel by car or airplane, talk on the phone, or watch television.

Although extremely profitable, the industry has endured some upheavals: In early 1999, oil prices dropped below $10 per barrel—the lowest level since before the oil crises of the 1970s—due to a global petroleum surplus. While prices did recover, the plunge meant a lot of sleepless nights in so-called Oil Patch cities like Houston and New Orleans, with oil equipment and services companies taking a particularly hard hit. Then, in 2001, rising energy prices caused power crises, especially in California—resulting in more regulatory attention being paid to energy companies. Also in 2001, high-flying energy broker Enron became a spectacular failure, going bankrupt, laying off thousands, and watching in horror as its value tumbled and company officers came under legal scrutiny for alleged shady dealings; the entire energy-trading sector has slowed as a result of this and other alleged corporate malfeasance.

Conflicting forces will shape the future of the energy industry. Deregulation, initiated by the 1992 National Energy Policy Act, is transforming energy companies from regulated monopolies to free-market competitors, changing the face of the utilities industry. Continuing expansion of industrial development across the planet will spur increased global consumption of energy. However, that will cause worsening pollution and the depletion of natural resources, raising the question: can we continue using energy as we have been? Perhaps not.

Some energy policies already foreshadow changes, an example being new, stringent EPA regulations in the United States. In the near term, though, neither environmental concerns nor volatile oil prices are likely to threaten the U.S. energy and utilities industry's role as a major supplier to the world market. It enjoys annual revenues of hundreds of billions of dollars and a demand that could double by 2020.

Trends

War: What is it good for? Higher oil prices. That's what it's good for. Standard & Poor's estimated in 2002 that the recent crisis in the Middle East added $4 to $7 to the price of each barrel of crude oil. And with the Bush administration taking military action against Saddam Hussein's Iraqi government, the price of oil has been pushed up even further. Which means higher prices at the pump—and bigger profits for oil companies.

Legal troubles. Enron isn't the only company looking at legal troubles. Others like Dynegy and CMS Energy are under investigation due to their round-trip energy transactions. Allegedly, these companies artificially pumped up their revenue figures by engaging in these transactions.

New oilfields. Oil and gas may be dwindling resources in the long term, but in the short term there's plenty left in the ground to feed our need for energy. Currently companies are focused on finds in Brazil, the Soviet Union, West Africa, and the deep water in the Gulf of Mexico.

Playing politics. The oil companies don't retain armies of lawyers and lobbyists—or make huge political contributions—for nothing. With strong ecological arguments existing against exploiting oil extraction in places like Alaska, the oil companies depend on legal and political clout to ensure they'll be able to continue exploiting oil finds. No example of the importance of political clout is better than Florida, home state of President Bush's brother, Governor Jeb Bush. The federal government recently agreed to purchase the rights to oil fields off the Gulf Coast of Florida from oil companies in order to prevent drilling there. Meanwhile, in California, environmentalists have been clamoring for decades for the government to do something similar to prevent drilling off the coast of that state; currently, there are signs the government may finally be ready to do for California what it did for Florida. But you can be sure the oil companies will do what they can to prevent that from coming to pass.

How It Breaks Down

America's energy companies are clustered in the Oil Patch region of Louisiana and East Texas, though many have major offices in Los Angeles and other coastal cities. The Big Oil companies are global; Exxon alone has a presence in some 100 countries. By contrast, utilities are generally more local in nature, usually doing business in a single city or region—though with deregulation, this is beginning to change. The vast industry can be broken down like this:

Integrated oil and natural gas. We have John D. Rockefeller and his Standard Oil Company to thank for the vertical integration of the world's largest oil and energy companies. His empire has long since been dispersed, but its legacy remains in the form of giants like Chevron, Exxon, and Phillips, which are involved in every phase of petroleum production and sales—from the extraction of crude oil through refining and shipping all the way up to the gas pump. Big Oil is a major force in the world's economy, but it is susceptible to global surpluses and plummeting oil prices when members of the Organization of Petroleum Exporting Countries (OPEC) cannot agree to restrain production.

Consumption and production of natural gas has grown far more rapidly in recent years partly due to its environmental advantage over oil. Also, natural gas is relatively less expensive as an electricity-generating fuel—an advantage that has been magnified by the competitive nature of the electricity industry since deregulation. While Big Oil is increasingly involved in the natural gas business, there are still specialists such as Questar Corporation.

Equipment and service. Companies like Schlumberger, Baker Hughes, and Halliburton provide the equipment and services that make it possible for the oil, coal, and gas companies to extract those products from Mother Earth. This once-booming sector took a hard hit in the late '90s due to over-production. While the largest companies will certainly survive, boutique concerns such as Dawson Geophysical (a technology expert) are more vulnerable.

Coal. Coal is primarily used for electricity generation and in a few manufacturing industries. It is increasingly in demand as developing countries such as China and India wire themselves for electricity. However, environmental

concerns may put a damper on the use of coal. The 1990 Clean Air Act called for cuts in high-sulfur coal production, and there are growing worries about global warming caused by burning fossil fuels. Even if coal consumption continues at current levels, reserves will last only another 200 years. Despite these concerns, the near-term future of coal production and consumption is bright. Major players in this arena include Arch Coal, the Peabody Group, and the Coastal Corporation.

Utilities. More than 3,000 utilities in the United States deliver electric power to individual homes and businesses. Major players include the Southern Company (the nation's largest investor-owned utility) as well as regional giants such as Public Service Energy Group in New Jersey, PECO Energy in Philadelphia, Pacific Gas and Electric in California, and Boston Edison in Massachusetts. The balance of the industry comprises federal agencies such as the Tennessee Valley Authority; local, publicly owned utilities, which are usually run by municipal or state agencies; and rural, nonprofit electric cooperatives, which serve small communities.

Nonutilities. Though they're in the business of electric power generation and distribution, nonutilities serve large individual clients—mostly utility companies that need extra electricity—as opposed to cities or regions. Though they only account for about ten percent of power generation, nonutilities—such as Nicor Energy, which is part of Nicor, Inc., and Duke Energy—represent the fastest-growing sector of the industry. In the wake of deregulation, smaller-scale generators are freer to sell energy to big distributors, and small, efficient producers can be quite profitable.

Key Jobs for MBAs

Project manager. For candidates who combine technical training with excellent business and communication skills, project management is the way to go. Stress levels can be high, but so are the pay and the sense of accomplishment that comes with the work. These jobs require at least a BS in engineering, as well as an MBA or an excellent industry track record.

Salary range: $90,000 to $200,000.

Marketer or public relations specialist. Marketing people must have a solid understanding of the client's energy needs, and of the utility or energy company's ability to meet them. Once again, candidates who combine technical and marketing backgrounds have the edge.

Salary range: $30,000 to $100,000.

Trade representative. Traditionally, people in these positions handled the sales of oil and other energy products in the futures markets. These days, electricity is becoming as much a commodity as oil; as a result, utilities now offer these types of positions as well. Candidates should have degrees in either engineering or business and marketing, plus proven negotiation or communication skills. People with both technology and MBA degrees can expect to do particularly well.

Salary range: $50,000 to $150,000.

Key Energy & Utilities Companies by 2002 Revenue

Company	Revenue ($M)	% Change from 2001	# of Employees
Royal Dutch/Shell Group	179,431	33	111,000
Exxon Mobil	178,909	−5	92,500
ChevronTexaco	91,685	−66	53,014
ConocoPhillips	50,512	110	57,000
Marathon Oil	30,595	−8	28,166
Valero Energy Corp.	26,976	80	19,947
Duke Energy	15,663	−74	22,000
Exelon	14,955	−1	25,200
American Electric Power Co.	14,555	−76	22,083
Halliburton Co.	12,498	−3	83,000
PG&E	12,495	−46	21,814
Sunoco	12,465	1	14,000
El Paso	12,194	−79	11,855
FirstEnergy	12,152	−52	17,560
Amerada Hess Corp.	11,932	−11	11,662
Edison Int'l	11,488	−1	15,038
Southern Co.	10,549	4	26,178
Dominion Resources	10,218	−3	17,000
TXU Corp.	10,034	−64	14,600
Xcel Energy	9,524	−35	14,642
Consolidated Edison	8,482	−12	14,293
Public Svc Enterprise Group	8,390	−15	12,911
CenterPoint Energy	7,922	−83	12,019

Continued next page

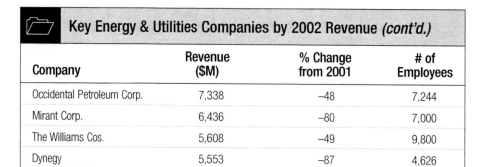

Key Energy & Utilities Companies by 2002 Revenue *(cont'd.)*			
Company	Revenue ($M)	% Change from 2001	# of Employees
Occidental Petroleum Corp.	7,338	−48	7,244
Mirant Corp.	6,436	−80	7,000
The Williams Cos.	5,608	−49	9,800
Dynegy	5,553	−87	4,626
Sources: Fortune.com; Hoovers.com; WetFeet analysis.			

Additional Resources

American Gas Association (http://www.aga.org)

Center for Energy and Economic Development (http://www.ceednet.org)

Energy Crossroads
(http://eetd.lbl.gov/EnergyCrossroads/EnergyCrossroads.html)

Energy Information Administration (http://www.eia.doe.gov)

Hoover's Energy Industry Snapshot
(http://www.hoovers.com/industry/snapshot/profile/0,3519,16,00.html)

Hoover's Utilities Industry Snapshot
(http://www.hoovers.com/industry/snapshot/profile/0,3519,48,00.html)

McKinsey Quarterly: Energy
http://www.mckinseyquarterly.com/category_editor.asp?L2=8)

Oil and Gas Journal (http://ogj.pennnet.com/cd_anchor_home)

Platts Global Energy (http://www.platts.com/)

Enterprise Software

Industry Overview

In the beginning was the mainframe, but it was slow and clunky. Then there was the departmental network, but it was not connected to anything else. Then there was the enterprise software company, which called this disconnectedness "islands of automation" and promised productivity gains by linking departments together. And it came to pass. And lo, it was good. Sometimes.

At its broadest, ERP (Enterprise Resource Planning) software is the segment of the software industry that serves the information needs of entire enterprises, including very large corporations with offices around the world. ERP software companies take information that is used throughout a company and put it into databases. They create software that allows people throughout the company to gain access to those databases. They help the company buy and install hardware on which the databases reside and the software runs. They offer consulting help in changing company procedures to get maximum benefit out of all this computerization of information. Software, hardware, databases, and procedures, taken together, constitute an ERP system.

Used mostly by mid- to large-sized companies, ERP systems let companies exchange key data among management, HR, finance, and operational departments, and with both suppliers and customers. In theory, and often in fact, this produces both better-informed management, more efficient operations, lower costs, and higher profits.

Each ERP system is tailor-made for the company it serves. This means that the ERP world is very different from its cousin, the consumer software (sometimes called packaged software) market. Consumer software often sells for less than $100 dollars and can be installed by the user with little trouble. ERP software, on the other hand, carries a six- or seven-figure price tag and takes as long as a year for trained professionals to install and customize.

Companies take months to determine an ERP budget, decide what they need an ERP system to do, and choose a vendor. The process results in a long sales cycle, often taking more than a year. Good sales people know as much about a client's internal politics as about its IT needs. According to one insider, ERP vendors sell a relationship as much as a product: "Companies choose the people they like best, not always the best product."

Currently, the emphasis in ERP is shifting from making new sales to servicing installed systems. ERP vendors have found that the service business can bring in three to seven times the software-licensing fees. Such services include training users, taking on the maintenance of a client's system, and most lucratively, implementing and customizing the software, though all the major vendors rely on information technology consulting firms to do the bulk of the work.

Trends

Cross-vendor integration. Since it's difficult for one vendor to provide everything a client needs in the way of enterprise functionality, companies often employ several vendors to fill all their enterprise-software needs. For example, a company may need to turn to different vendors for ERP, CRM (customer resource management), supply-chain, and employee-recruiting software. With this variety

of software, compatibility issues arise. Recently, the major enterprise-software suppliers have begun to develop interoperability standards for integration of their products at the business process level.

New market development. The market for enterprise software has traditionally consisted of large, multinational corporations who could afford it and whose operations were on a scale to realize big economies from implementing enterprise software. But as the enterprise-software market has grown, new small vendors have seen an opportunity. Using new technology and products requiring less customization, they are finding less expensive ways to deliver enterprise solutions, making it affordable for a wider range of smaller clients.

Shift in emphasis in ERP. Currently, the emphasis in ERP is shifting from making new sales to servicing installed systems. ERP vendors have found that the service business can bring in three to seven times the software-licensing fees. Such services include training users, taking on the maintenance of a client's system, and implementing and customizing the software (which is the most lucrative), though all the major vendors rely on information technology consulting firms to do the bulk of the work.

Business analytics (or business intelligence). This new sector of the enterprise-software industry shows real promise. Where ERP systems are focused primarily on lowering costs via better allocation of internal resources, business analytics software aims to pump up revenue. These systems sift through mountains of data to help companies maximize sales performance down to the individual-product level—for instance, by suggesting a new pricing level for a product line to maximize the revenue attached to it. Players in this segment include Business Objects, SAI Institute, and Cognos.

How It Breaks Down

Most observers break down the industry according to size, as follows:

Tier 1 players. The Big Four—Baan, Oracle, PeopleSoft, and SAP—are full-service, multinational vendors that create software suites—covering everything from payroll to manufacturing and distribution to company financials—tailored for specific industries. Increasingly, they implement the software, train users, and maintain and upgrade systems.

Tier 2 players. These smaller players tend to focus on one functional area—HR, for example—and tailor the product for only a few industries, though some have the same scope as the Big Four, just with much less market share. Examples of solid tier 2 companies are J.D. Edwards, a software-suite vendor that sometimes is put in the same category as the Big Four (in which case it becomes the Big Five); Siebel Systems, a CRM software provider, and Manugistics, a supply chain management specialist.

Tier 3 players. These are primarily startups that tend to focus on niche areas of the ERP market, hoping to fill needs that the Big Four have overlooked. Approaches vary: for example, Convoy develops software that complements that of ERP heavyweight PeopleSoft, while Employease spars with PeopleSoft in the human resources ring.

Consulting firms. Apart from the vendors, there are also the partners—Big Five and former Big Five consulting firms (Accenture, Deloitte Consulting, Cap Gemini Ernst & Young, BearingPoint) as well as IBM Business Consulting Services, which acquired PwC Consulting and smaller consulting firms that help implement ERP software and integrate it with clients' preexisting (or legacy)

systems. Implementation is where the big bucks in ERP are, since it takes months for consultants to customize software to the end users' needs.

Key Jobs for MBAs

Jobs fall into two general areas: technical and nontechnical, or business. About 80 percent of the jobs in this industry are on the technical side. Salary levels listed below are base salaries only; compensation generally exceeds the base.

Implementation consultant. Consultants are the shock troops with the technical and business know-how to implement the software and customize it to fit a client's particular business needs. Most work is done on client sites, working in close contact with clients in projects that can last from a few months to more than a year.

Salary range: $40,000 to $60,000 to start; senior consultants make well into six figures.

Sales manager. Sales in ERP is a little different than sales in other industries, particularly consumer software. Although you will need to keep very focused on customer needs and wants, the dollars involved mean that the sales cycle is longer, more technical, and may often involve custom solutions. In-depth knowledge of both the product and the client's business issues are essential, so perience with ERP software and lots of sales experience are usually prerequisites.

Salary range: $45,000 to $80,000 base pay; meeting quotas will earn you your base pay figure again in bonus, and exceeding quotas will earn you multiples of your salary.

Key Enterprise Software Companies by 2002 Revenue

Company	Revenue ($M)	% Change from 2001	# of Employees
Invensys	9,939	−11	73,005
Oracle	9,673	−11	42,006
SAP	7,786	19	28,878
Computer Associates Int'l	3,116	5	16,600
PeopleSoft	1,949	−6	8,293
Siebel Systems	1,635	−20	5,909
BMC Software	1,327	3	6,335
J.D. Edwards & Co.	905	4	4,954
Cognos	491	−1	2,600
Hyperion Solutions Corp.	492	−5	2,252
Business Objects	455	9	2,162
Aspen Technology	321	3	2,200
Manugistics Group	272	−12	1,384
WebMethods	196	−3	888
Informatica	195	−1	796
QAD	195	−4	1,325

Sources: Hoovers.com; WetFeet analysis.

Additional Resources

BRINT.com (http://www.brint.com)

ComputerWorld (http://www.computerworld.com)

ERP Fan Club and User Forum (http://www.erpfans.com)

International Data Corporation (http://www.idc.com)

Internet World (http://www.internetworld.com)

Entertainment & Sports

Industry Overview

In entertainment and sports, the profits come from discretionary spending, so these industries enjoy the most success in economically stable countries where leisure dollars flow freely. Industry companies supply their audiences with large-scale sporting events, music concerts, TV situation comedies, and silver-screen masterpieces. Simply put, they're in the business of fun.

Even during economically depressed periods, this industry flourishes as an escape from hard times—for all walks of life. And standing at the pinnacle of entertainment culture are the celebrities: the movie stars and quarterbacks and rock stars and talk-show hostesses who seem to realize our dreams and thereby

give us hope. This is the only industry whose product is an illusion—neither a good nor a service, and yet both at the same time.

The culture in this industry is one of anti-corporate, studied casualness. There are still uniforms—an ever-changing array of baseball caps and jackets in the music business, for example. But they're invariably less starchy, more expressive of individualism, than anything worn to work in the fields of finance or law. The people? Well, there's no people like show people, and the sports world has even more pep. This is a high-energy crowd. It's also a big-ego crowd, and working with its members can be both stimulating and frustrating.

Bottom line, though, is that even if your job does not bring you into contact with the creative members of the industry, the glamour rubs off, lending an aura of excitement to mundane tasks that would be boring in any other industry. Poring over Nielsen ratings all day doesn't sound so bad when you describe it to your dinner companions as analyzing the relative sex appeal of Jerry Springer, Oprah Winfrey, and Dan Rather.

Trends

Vertical integration. A few enormous conglomerates dominate the entire entertainment industry, each controlling television, film, publishing, new media, and music businesses under one umbrella. Often, they own professional sports franchises as part of the package. Congress has encouraged this integration by easing restrictions on how many television stations one company can own and by passing the 1996 Telecommunications Act, which lifted an important ban on telecom companies developing new media content.

At the same time, technological developments are leading to a convergence of digital television, digital audio systems, and the Internet, so that all home entertainment may soon be distributed through a single so-called set-top box, as

simply as MP3 music files are now distributed over the Internet. If you are interested in this industry, watch for unexpected potential employers such as Microsoft and Intel, companies that are expected to play major roles in the industry's development.

War for control of copyrighted entertainment products. The fight against Napster, an online music file-swapping application, was just the beginning of the entertainment industry's efforts to make sure it doesn't lose profits due to new technologies that allow consumers to access entertainment products without paying for them.

In terms of online music file sharing, the industry has now turned its sights on technologies such as those offered by KaZaa and Audiogalaxy, hoping to prevent them from allowing the sharing of copyrighted songs. In addition to citing the legal protections due to copyrighted materials and initiating legal battles with file-sharing providers, some big entertainment companies have resorted to taking over or partnering with these companies to ensure they make money from the sharing of copyrighted files: BMG, for instance, partnered with Napster, and Vivendi took over MP3. Others are banding together to provide their own online services: AOL, EMI, and Bertelsmann, for instance, formed MusicNet. And a good chunk of new music products these days come with copyright-protection software that limits users' abilities to copy files.

In the broader fight to make money off all use of copyrighted entertainment products, the industry is now trying to make the case that all PCs and other digital products that run entertainment software should come loaded with software "keys" that will "unlock" software protections embedded in the industry's digital products. File-sharing advocates point to the rise of the VCR market as evidence that the industry is misguided in its efforts; Despite the movie industry's howls of protest when VCRs came on the market some 20 years ago, VCR technology ended up vastly increasing consumption of the industry's products—and pumped up profits in the process.

New television landscape. In the old days, the major networks—ABC, NBC, and CBS—ruled the television roost. Nowadays, cable channels (everything from HBO to MTV to Comedy Central) make for a much more fragmented landscape. Adding to the confusion has been the success of upstart networks like Fox, UPN, and the WB. To enhance their moneymaking ability, the major networks have adopted an "if you can't beat 'em, join 'em" strategy, making all kinds of production and distribution agreements with their cable competition.

How It Breaks Down

Despite the blurring lines between sports, music, movies, cable, and publishing—and the media behemoths that preside over them all—these various forms of entertainment are distinct domains. And though at Time Warner you could conceivably enjoy a career that includes working for the Atlanta Braves, Home Box Office, Six Flags theme parks, and the Atlantic record label, most people choose one area and stick with it. These worlds are closely knit, and whom you know and whom you owe—and who owes you—counts for a great deal, particularly when you're looking for work.

Film. In the days of celluloid movie factories, the major studios controlled the project from the earliest script draft to the opening night at Radio City. Most films were completed in under a month and cost as little as $200,000 to produce. Today there are six major entertainment companies: News Corp, AOL Time Warner, Vivendi, Sony, Viacom, and Walt Disney. Known as the Big Six, they all have their roots in the original Hollywood studios: MGM, Warner Brothers, Paramount, and others. But the modern studios control Hollywood in a different way now: They solicit projects, provide the financing, and make the deals with thousands of smaller production companies. The indies (independents) remain only marginally profitable—and are often owned by one of the Big Six. (Miramax, e.g., is a Disney subsidiary.)

Music. Like most movies, music is often created by committee and on the whim of the record label. But the artists retain some control. At least, some do; the Billboard charts always seem to have room for packaged products like Menudo, the Monkees, and N'Sync. The 1996 Telecommunications Act lifted restrictions on how many radio stations a company can own and the ensuing domination by conglomerates resulted in more standardized (and oft-criticized) playlists nationwide.

Beyond the Top 40, music is also big business in conjunction with the advertising industry: Whoever owns the rights to songs used in big national ad campaigns stands a good chance of making even more than the record company or the artist. Sony is currently the acknowledged leader in the business. Other top music companies are Time Warner (Atlantic), EMI (Virgin, Capitol), Vivendi (PolyGram, Universal), and Bertelsmann (Arista, RCA).

Television. The old news in television is the emergence of cable, the decline in network viewership, and the surprising success of Fox TV, the only new network to date that has threatened the supremacy of reigning giants CBS, NBC, and ABC. The more interesting and pertinent news for job seekers is the slow but inexorable digital convergence of computer technology, the Internet, and television, and also the 1996 Telecommunications Act, which allows phone companies and power utilities, among others, to create and distribute entertainment content. These developments opened the floodgates for telecommunications and technology companies to enter the competition—Pacific Telesis (NYNEX and SBC), AT&T (TCI), Intel, and Compaq have become strong players. Also building on this technology, Microsoft and other companies are melding broadband cable and electronic media to enhance Internet capabilities.

Sports. When world-class athletes cry, "Show me the money," team owners, managers, agents, and sponsors dance to the tune. The popularity of professional sports teams is phenomenal, and sky-high revenues are pulled in through a variety of avenues including advertising, sponsorships, team name and logo licensing, ticket sales, and worldwide broadcasts.

As far as professional organizations go, the National Football League (NFL) leads the pack in profits, with the National Basketball Association (NBA), Major League Baseball (MLB), and the National Hockey League (NHL) not far behind. Teams, once owned by individuals, are increasingly owned by companies: AOL Time Warner (publisher of Sports Illustrated) owns baseball's Atlanta Braves, basketball's Atlanta Hawks, and hockey's Atlanta Thrashers; the Tribune Company owns baseball's Chicago Cubs; Walt Disney owns hockey's Mighty Ducks of Anaheim and baseball's Anaheim Angels; and News Corp., Cablevision, Comcast, The Molson Companies, and Anheuser-Busch all have teams as well.

Key Jobs for MBAs

Marketing and promotion. These are perhaps the most transferable of all skill sets in this business. Vast and constant infusions of market analysis, research, writing, graphics, and well-organized planning and distribution support every important sports event, hit song, new television show, and box-office gamble. Being an account executive or marketing manager is also great training for whatever senior executive role you may ultimately want to play in one of these entertainment engines. The gas they all run on is marketing and promotion. Learn how to do it effectively and well and you'll always have work.

Salary range: $40,000 to $110,000.

Key Entertainment Companies by 2002 Revenue

Company	Revenue ($M)	% Change from 2001	# of Employees
AOL Time Warner	40,961	7	91,250
Walt Disney	25,329	0	112,000
Viacom	24,606	6	120,630
Bertelsmann	19,193	13	80,632
Sony Corp. of America	18,557	8	22,000
The News Corp.	16,344	25	33,800
Warner Bros. Entertainment	10,040	46	31,200
ABC	9,763	2	n/a
Fox Entertainment	9,725	14	12,800
Clear Channel	8,421	6	41,800
CBS	7,490	4	n/a
NBC	7,149	24	n/a
Vivendi Universal	6,572	50	20,000
USA Interactive	4,621	33	23,200
National Football League*	4,200	17	450
Major League Baseball*	3,500	10	n/a
EMI Group	3,487	−8	9,270
NASCAR	3,000	20	450
DreamWorks SKG	2,219	19	1,500
National Basketball Assn**	2,164	n/a	n/a
National Hockey League**	1,697	15	n/a
Metro-Goldwyn-Mayer	1,654	19	1,150
LucasFilm*	1,500	36	2,000
BMG Entertainment	1,467	−68	9,758
AMC Entertainment	1,342	10	17,700

*2001 figures; **2000 figures. Sources: Hoovers.com; WetFeet analysis.

Additional Resources

Billboard (http://www.billboard.com)

EntertainmentCareers.net (http://www.entertainmentcareers.net)

Hollywood Reporter (http://www.hollywoodreporter.com)

Hoover's TV & Radio Industry Snapshot
(http://www.hoovers.com/industry/snapshot/profile/0,3519,40,00.html)

Hoover's Movies & Music Industry Snapshot
(http://www.hoovers.com/industry/snapshot/profile/0,3519,30,00.html)

McKinsey Quarterly: Media and Entertainment
(http://www.mckinseyquarterly.com/category_editor.asp?L2=17)

Work in Sports (http://www.workinsports.com/home.asp)

Health Care

Industry Overview

Although this line of work probably interests you because of its humanitarian and service aspects, the industry as a whole—hospitals, nursing homes, home health care, specialized clinics, and nontraditional options such as homeopathic treatment—is all business these days. That said, the business of health care is booming. It's estimated that in 2002, the United States spent a whopping $1.37 trillion on health care—almost 14 percent of the gross domestic product.

The health care industry provides diagnostic, healing, rehabilitation, and prevention services for the injured, ailing, incapacitated, and disabled. The individual physician is its first line of contact with consumers. However, the health care organization—the hospital or health management organization (HMO)—is the conduit of insurance payments, which form the preponderance of the industry's, and the physician's, revenues. The lion's share of these revenues comes from employee health insurance plans, Medicare (health insurance for Americans over the age of 65), and Medicaid (health insurance for Americans on welfare). Health care organizations, except for county hospitals, are usually run for profit. This creates tension between doctors who want to prescribe expensive treatments and diagnostic tests and health care organizations, which want to cut costs.

There are an abundance of opportunities for people interested in health care—whether or not you have an MD (or even a bachelor's degree). As of December 2001, more than ten million people nationwide worked in the health care service industry. That number will only rise as people are living longer and

needing more preventative and long-term care. The demand for health care workers is expected to grow faster than the average rate of increase for all other occupations until 2010. Statistics indicate a growing need for home care aides, registered nurses, physician assistants, nurse practitioners, physical therapists, nontraditional health aides, and physicians. Not to mention all of the technical and administrative jobs that are in high demand as hospitals focus their energies on efficient management and profitability.

Trends

Cost tensions. There are some major tensions in the industry between forces that want to lower costs and forces that have the effect of raising costs. On the one hand, payers (primarily insurance companies, HMOs, and the government) have reduced their reimbursements for various medical services, and health care providers have become much more careful about disbursing services. On the other hand, there are new drugs and new procedures that can help patients like never before, political pressures to treat patients better via better medical care and patient privacy, and a tremendous labor shortage (primarily of nurses and medical technicians), which health care organizations are trying to address—all of which costs money. In addition, an aging Baby Boomer population is making for greater demand than ever for quality medical care. Managing these tensions is a key issue for the industry these days.

Cardiac care. One of the areas of the industry with the most impressive advances in recent years has been cardiac care. Advances in products like defibrillators and artificial hearts have made cardiac care more effective than ever before. Companies like ZOLL Medical, Cardiac Science, ABIOMED, and World Heart are among those that focus on making these kinds of devices.

How It Breaks Down

Hospitals. Despite the increased outsourcing of medical records, housekeeping, lab testing, and clinical services like orthopedics and radiology, hospitals are still the biggest employers in the health care industry. The huge networks such as HCA and Tenet need a steady supply of doctors, nurses, administrators, medical technicians, therapists, and other support staff. In areas where competition from HMOs is mounting and cost cutting is a priority, former staff may move outside the immediate confines of a hospital. However, close and important links remain—particularly for any type of surgery or specialized treatment like chemotherapy.

HMOs and PPOs. Health maintenance organizations and preferred provider organizations are hybrids between a hospital and an insurance company. Each type of managed care plan covers primary care visits, preventative services, and copayments for prescription drugs, while only PPOs allow the enrollee to choose his or her physician (HMOs maintain a list of plan-approved doctors). Some of the largest organizations actually have their own medical staffs and facilities at which they treat patients; smaller ones may just access networks of private providers and hospitals. Competition is fierce in this arena—mergers, acquisitions, and internal strife often destabilize the job market. Coventry, Humana, Harvard Pilgrim Health Care, Group Health Cooperative, and Pacificare (one of the leading Medicare HMOs) are a few of the better-known players.

Specialty providers. As hospitals have attempted to cut costs, they have turned to firms that can provide specialized services at rock-bottom prices. These include everything from nursing homes (Beverly Enterprises) to home infusion therapy providers (Apria Healthcare) to diabetes treatment providers (American

Healthways). Clinics that focus on special treatments such as chemotherapy, MRIs, and other scanning techniques, and physical therapy for the handicapped are also proliferating. Most are small and locally run, but Gambro and FFresenius Medical Care are two enormous service companies that focus on this type of care; more will undoubtedly emerge as their popularity increases.

Home care. Advances in technology have done much to improve efficiency and reduce costs for both patients and home care staff. Today, home care nurses and aides can administer complex treatments, previously only available in hospitals or clinics, to the elderly and severely disabled in their own homes. And because almost all hospitals and HMOs now release patients before they are self-sufficient, home care is often the most viable choice. Most jobs in this sector don't require much training (they are closely supervised by an RN, NP, or physician), just deep reserves of patience and kindness. But the pay is low—often under $10 an hour—and the work is arduous. The rewards? Hours are extremely flexible, and there is plenty of personal contact with clients.

Key Jobs for MBAs

Health care managers. These are the jobs where an MBA comes in handy and a background in cost cutting, marketing, and information management will give you an edge over the competition. Lots of people want these jobs, and though industry observers predict that the number of managerial slots in hospitals and HMOs will shrink to perhaps half the current number, the need for qualified executive staff in home health care, nursing homes, and clinics is expected to more than make up the difference.

Salary range: $55,000 and up. Experienced managers with an impressive track record in meeting and maintaining strict budgets can earn well over six figures.

Key Health Care Organizations by 2002 Revenue

Company	Revenue ($M)	% Change from 2001	# of Employees
Blue Cross*	143,200	14	150,000
Cardinal Health	51,136	6	50,000
McKesson	50,006	19	24,000
AmerisourceBergen	45,235	179	13,700
UnitedHealth Group	25,020	8	32,000
Kaiser Foundation	22,500	14	125,000
Aetna	19,879	−21	28,000
HCA	19,729	10	178,000
Cigna	19,348	1	41,200
WellPoint Health Networks	17,024	40	16,200
AdvancePCS	13,107	87	5,655
Anthem	13,282	27	19,500
Express Scripts	12,261	31	7,561
Humana	11,175	11	13,500
PacifiCare Health System	10,894	−6	7,800
Health Net	10,149	2	9,400
Tenet Healthcare Corp.	8,743	−28	113,877
Baxter Int'l	8,110	6	54,600
Caremark Rx	6,805	21	4,723
Medtronic	6,411	16	28,000
Fresenius Medical Care	5,084	5	37,000
Oxford Health Plans	4,963	12	3,500
HEALTHSOUTH Corp.	4,311	−2	51,000
Becton, Dickinson & Co.	4,033	7	25,249
Owens & Minor	3,960	4	2,968

Continued next page

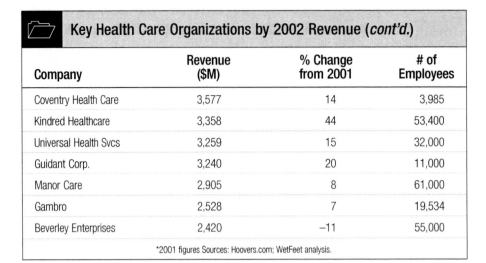

Key Health Care Organizations by 2002 Revenue (*cont'd.*)

Company	Revenue ($M)	% Change from 2001	# of Employees
Coventry Health Care	3,577	14	3,985
Kindred Healthcare	3,358	44	53,400
Universal Health Svcs	3,259	15	32,000
Guidant Corp.	3,240	20	11,000
Manor Care	2,905	8	61,000
Gambro	2,528	7	19,534
Beverley Enterprises	2,420	−11	55,000

*2001 figures Sources: Hoovers.com; WetFeet analysis.

Additional Resources

Agency for Healthcare Research and Quality (http://www.ahcpr.gov)

Hoover's Medical Equipment Industry Snapshot
(http://www.hoovers.com/industry/snapshot/profile/0,3519,56,00.html)

Hoover's Health Care Services Industry Snapshot
(http://www.hoovers.com/industry/snapshot/profile/0,3519,23,00.html)

InPharm.com (http://www.inpharm.com)

Knowledge @ Wharton: Health Economics
(http://knowledge.wharton.upenn.edu/category.cfm?catid=6)

McKinsey Quarterly: Health Care
(http://www.mckinseyquarterly.com/category_editor.asp?L2=12)

WetFeet®

Internet & New Media

Industry Overview

Trying ardently to fulfill the promise of the Web, Internet companies—start-ups as well as online extensions of clicks-and-mortar companies—have singled out some activity to reinvent by conducting it on the Internet—distributing textbooks, software, or greeting cards; disseminating medical information, fiction, or law school classes; planning parties; or swapping vacation homes. For all of these activities, and many more, the Internet makes it possible to distribute information of all kinds and conduct a transaction at the same time, anywhere in the world, immediately.

In the process, companies are doing a stunningly wide variety of things online—selling products, producing newspaper- and magazine-style publications, providing services like travel agencies and stock brokerages, delivering search engines, recruiting employees, building brands, and developing online gaming networks, to name a few. Add to this all of the companies that underpin and service these endeavors—the online ad agencies, Internet service providers (ISPs), and management consultancies—and you get a sense of just how broad this industry is.

In the past couple of years, Internet companies have witnessed a precipitous decline in advertising revenue. As a result, many pure-play Internet companies have gone under, and some old-economy companies decided to scale back their Web operations, leaving tens of thousands of people out of work. What happened? It turns out that many of the biggest online advertising spenders happened to be the struggling Internet companies themselves. Quick money

from cash-rich dot coms willing to wantonly spend for market share and brand awareness is gone. And old-economy companies facing cost-cutting pressures in a difficult economic environment became less likely to spend for online advertising. The result: a dried-up revenue stream, and hard times for Internet companies with an advertising revenue model. Even behemoths like Yahoo! and AOL Time Warner have been hit hard.

In the new world order, Internet companies must demonstrate profitability or a clear plan for it, or risk near-term financial disaster. In other words, to make it on the Web these days, you'd better have a strong e-commerce component, or at least a viable subscription model if you're primarily a content provider.

In the case of public Internet companies, the majority have disappointed stakeholders with lower revenues and longer than projected "paths to profitability." As far as the remaining private start-up shops are concerned, most are very short on cash; the much-needed venture capital funding no longer flows freely. The result: Either companies fold or scale back considerably. For most pure-play Internet companies, an IPO is no longer a viable exit strategy.

Trends

Layoffs and closed shops. The harsh realities of the economic decline, budget cuts, hiring freezes, and, worst of all, layoffs, have hit the Internet industry hard. Such cost-cutting actions are nothing new to corporate veterans, but have become painful lessons to the new, younger generation of dot-com workers. Often in droves, and more often without warning, tech firms are asking employees to leave in order to trim their costs. Each month the unemployment rate seems to reach a new high. Marketing and content jobs have been slashed the most. Safest are techies and salespeople, though even they can face the ax.

And if a company closes its doors—as many have in recent times—everybody is out of a job, no matter what his or her job title.

Bright spots. The Internet seems to work best, from a business perspective, for companies engaged in low-overhead e-commerce—for instance, financial, software, and travel-services sites that don't deal in storing or shipping inventory have low costs once they've established their technological infrastructure. For example, Expedia, a leading travel site, operates on a 70 percent profit margin. Amazon.com, on the other hand—which has to deal with procuring and shipping actual physical products—operates at a 26 percent margin.

Blog-a-thon. Back in the 1990s, Web pundits hyped the ability of the Internet to bring people together on a one-to-many basis—to give Internet users a voice they didn't have previously, and thus make the world a smaller place. It might not be doing quite that, but the promise of one-to-many connections is being fulfilled these days by the weblog phenomenon. Weblogs—"blogs," for short—are a kind of online diary, in which the author, or "blogger," writes regular postings about whatever interests him or her, often including hyperlinks to other Web pages containing information about the topic at hand. Now Web pundits are making the claim that blogs are going to change the face of journalism; again, we'll have to wait and see on that claim. But there's no doubt blogs are proliferating—and that even journalists and newspapers are getting in on the act.

How It Breaks Down

The industry is a baggy monster that resists classification. The following breakdown is not a definitive taxonomy but rather a chance for the uninitiated to make some sense of a rapidly changing landscape.

Publishers. Online publications make money by selling advertising or subscriptions or both. Most of the players are losing money, and widespread profitability seems unlikely in the near future. Many players in this field are online ventures of already-established media brands. Some examples include the Wall Street Journal Interactive Edition, a subscription-based version of the leading business newspaper; and ESPN.com, an extension of the sports cable channel.

There are also a number of important players whose primary presence is online. A few examples are CNet, which provides news and information on the online world, and CitySearch, which is actually a cluster of publications, each devoted to life (restaurants, movies, community-service opportunities, and so on) in a given city. And hundreds of daily newspapers put all or part of their content on websites that are still exploring the differences between reporting for print and for the Web.

Vendors. Vendors make money by selling goods or services. The best-known online seller of goods is Amazon.com. Mail-order companies with websites—Lands' End, for example—fall into this category. Other sellers provide services: E*TRADE and Charles Schwab act as stockbrokers, Expedia acts as a travel agent, and FreeMarkets creates customized business-to-business online auctions for large buyers of industrial parts, raw materials, and commodities.

Aggregators and portals. Some of the busiest sites on the Web fall into this category. Search engines—which account for five of the ten busiest websites—are aggregators (so named because they offer a huge aggregation of links to other websites). Portals (also known as gateways or start pages) are sites that serve as home base for Web surfers. The home page of AOL, for example, is designed as an Internet portal. In a move that typifies the fluidity and opportunism of this industry, the leading search engines, such as Yahoo!, have positioned themselves as gateways, and vice versa. Other so-called freestanding

search engines like the popular Google.com have opted for search performance over the glitz and glam of gateways.

All of these sites make money from banner advertising (think billboards on your computer screen) or, increasingly, through alliances with companies that pay a lot of money to be the gateway or aggregator's "preferred provider" of travel services, greeting cards, and so on.

Communities. Online communities serve as centers for people who share special interests. GeoCities is one of the largest, hosting a number of communities with interests as varied as fashion, golf, and government. Other examples of community sites include Motley Fool for small investors; BabyCenter, a site for parents; iVillage, a site for women; and PlanetOut, a site for gays and lesbians. All of these sites encourage users to sign up for free memberships by offering access to chat, newsletters, and bulletin boards; some offer members the opportunity to construct Web pages, which then reside in the community's site and serve as a draw for more members. Like many other Internet concerns, these sites used to make money from advertising and alliances, but are trying to pump up revenue streams like e-commerce and subscriptions.

Consulting and support. This category encompasses all of the companies that have sprung up to support and provide services to the industry. The ISP (Internet service provider) world is still divided between large players like America Online and smaller local players, although many of the latter are being bought and consolidated into national companies. Most of the major phone companies are also competing as ISPs. Local and long distance carriers such as PacBell and AT&T provide the latest in DSL and high-speed cable Internet connections.

This segment also includes a variety of now-struggling consulting firms that help develop websites, providing services including management and strategic

consulting specialized for Web companies, online advertising, e-commerce development, user-interface design, and, increasingly, all of the above. Companies in this category include DiamondCluster International, Razorfish, Organic, and Sapient.

Key Jobs for MBAs

Project manager. The project manager (a.k.a. producer or product manager) acts to make sure that the various pieces of a multimedia puzzle—a website or a CD-ROM—are on track. This means making sure that the creative, technical, and business people are all in synch. Or as one job listing puts it, the producer "manages product from concept to final release, maintains product vision, and upholds business objectives." A project manager usually has substantial experience on the business or design side of things.

Salary range: $35,000 to $75,000.

Marketing associate or marketing director. In these positions, you'll conceive and execute advertising campaigns in the virtual and physical worlds. You'll also build a site's brand. Titles vary quite a bit in marketing, but the general idea is to drive people to a company's website, and then make money by selling products or subscriptions or whatever else the site sells. A college degree and good communications skills should be enough to land you a job in online marketing. Any previous marketing experience is helpful.

Salary range: $30,000 to $80,000.

Business development. Alliances and partnerships between and among sites are one of the driving features of online business. Business development folks identify possible partners, then negotiate and close deals and maintain relationships. MBAs tend to fit well in business development.

Salary range: $60,000 to $120,000.

Key Internet and New Media Companies by 2002 Revenue			
Company	Revenue ($M)	% Change from 2001	# of Employees
AOL Time Warner	40,961	7	91,250
Microsoft	28,365	12	50,500
Charles Schwab	4,480	−15	16,700
Amazon.com	3,933	26	7,500
E-Trade Group	1,910	−6	3,500
Priceline.com	1,004	−14	290
Earthlink	1,357	9	5,106
eBay	1,214	62	4,000
Monster	1,115	−23	8,500
Yahoo!	953	33	3,600
Ticketmaster	675	206	4,600
Terra Lycos	736	17	n/a
Ameritrade Holding Corp.	443	13	2,150
Travelocity.com*	302	57	1,554

*2001 figures. Sources: Hoovers.com; WetFeet analysis.

Additional Resources

Hoover's Internet Services Industry Snapshot
(http://www.hoovers.com/industry/snapshot/profile/0,3519,26,00.html)

Internet.com (http://www.internet.com/home-d.html)

Internet World (http://www.internetworld.com)

McKinsey Quarterly: E-Commerce
(http://www.mckinseyquarterly.com/category_editor.asp?L2=24)

Investment Banking

Industry Overview

Investment banks are experts at calculating what a business is worth, usually for one of two purposes: to price a securities offering or to set the value of a merger or acquisition. Securities include stocks and bonds, and a stock offering may be an initial public offering (IPO) or any subsequent (or *secondary*) offering. In both cases, I-banks charge hefty fees for providing this valuation service, along with other kinds of financial and business advice.

When banks underwrite stock or bond issues, they ensure that institutional investors, such as mutual funds or pension funds, commit to purchasing the issue of stocks or bonds before it actually hits the market. In this sense, I-banks are intermediaries between the issuers of securities and the investing public. I-banks make markets to facilitate securities trading by buying and selling securities out of their own account and profiting from the spread between the bid and the ask price. In addition, many I-banks offer retail brokerage (retail meaning the customers are individual investors rather than institutional investors) and asset management services.

Not surprisingly, the center of this industry rests in the lofty aeries above Wall Street and Midtown in New York City. Other hot spots include London, San Francisco, and Silicon Valley. Firms also compete in Frankfurt, Tokyo, Hong Kong, and other foreign markets 24 hours a day.

Industries

Trends

Cool down. As the global economic climate cools down, so has investment banking. IPO and M&A activity has all but dried up; the only bright spots on the Street are areas in which lower interest rates drive business, such as mortgage-backed and municipal securities. Meanwhile, the big banks have found themselves tremendously overstaffed, having hired new employees like gangbusters in the boom years of the 1990s. As a result, in the past couple of years, investment banks have laid off tens of thousands of employees. Reports vary, but some say employment levels are 25 percent lower than they were at their peak. At the same time, I-banking bonuses, which can comprise half or more of some employees' total annual compensation, have fallen by 50 percent or more. I-banks have also pulled back on college and MBA recruiting—but, because it's cheaper to employ a recent grad than someone with more experience, there are still jobs to be had for the cream of the crop from the best schools. More than ever, though, those who do I-banking internships will have the best shot at full-time openings.

Industry consolidation. Investment banking has witnessed a rash of cross-industry mergers and acquisitions in recent times, largely due to the late-1999 repeal of the Depression-era Glass-Steagall Act. The repeal, which marked the deregulation of the financial services industry, now allows commercial banks, investment banks, insurers, and securities brokerages to offer one another's services. As I-banks add retail brokerage and lending to their offerings and commercial banks try to build up their investment banking services, the industry is undergoing some serious global consolidation, allowing clients to invest, save, and protect their money all under one roof. These mergers have only added to the downward pressure on employment in the industry, as merged institutions make an effort to reduce redundancy. Among the M&A activity in recent years: First Boston and Donaldson, Lufkin & Jenrette were

both acquired by Credit Suisse; J.P. Morgan and Hambrecht & Quist were swallowed by Chase; Robertson Stephens was acquired by FleetBoston; and Alex. Brown was acquired by Deutsche Bank.

Meanwhile, foreign firms like Deutsche Bank and UBS are moving into U.S. markets aggressively. The result: Firms in the United States and abroad are looking for partners or acquisitions to beef up their global presence. "Almost everything we do now has some cross-border component. More than 50 percent of my work is in foreign investments," says one insider. "Every day I see a wire come across about something going on somewhere like Kenya or India."

Scandals on the street. The swing in the markets from up, up, up to down, down, down has focused a lot of scrutiny on firms on the Street. The biggest issue so far has been the fact that banks overrated the investment potential of client companies' stocks intentionally, deceiving investors in the pursuit of favorable relationships—and ongoing banking revenue opportunities—with those companies. Firms have also come under fire for the methods by which they allocated stock offerings (specifically, for whether they charged excessive commissions to clients who wanted to purchase hot offerings), as well as for possible manipulation of accounting rules in the course of presenting clients' financial info to potential investors.

To date, firms including Merrill Lynch, Credit Suisse First Boston, Citigroup, Goldman Sachs, Deutsche Bank, Bear Stearns, Morgan Stanley, J.P. Morgan Chase, and UBS Warburg—in other words, everybody who's anybody on the Street—have paid fines totaling in the billions of dollars to settle allegations against them, and the scrutiny of regulators remains sharp, with more fines sure to come. In addition, big-time players on the Street, including research analysts like Henry Blodget (Merrill Lynch) and Jack Grubman (Citigroup) and bankers like Frank Quattrone (CSFB) have been accused of misdeeds and/or fined and

fired. However, it's important to realize that to behemoth institutions like the bulge bracket banks, these fines are a drop in the bucket when compared to their total annual revenues. After all, regulators don't want to destroy the big banks—they're too central to the global economy. Whether the slap-on-the-wrist approach will result in permanent changes to the way banks do business remains to be seen.

New relationships between research and banking. All that said, several changes in the way banks do business seem sure, all of them relating to research: less of a link between research analysts' compensation and firms' banking revenues, less of a role for research analysts in seeking banking business, and more objectivity in research reports. Already, banks are enforcing new degrees of separation between bankers and research analysts: As part of a settlement with New York, Merrill Lynch agreed to strengthen the barriers between research and banking; and Citigroup has spun off its research department into a distinct company (named Smith Barney). The SEC is now requiring research analysts to affirm in writing that the recommendations in their reports are truly what they believe, and that they have received no payment for specific research opinions (a requirement designed to de-link research analysts' compensation from their firms' banking efforts).

The tricky thing about all this is that separating research from banking makes it harder for banks to justify the costs of conducting research. Without revenues that are directly or indirectly the result of their research departments, research becomes purely a cost center. As a result, banks are likely to look to cut costs in research moving forward. That means research departments will either have to cover fewer companies or cover a greater number of companies per analyst—or both. Indeed, in the spring of 2003 Citigroup announced that it is ending its coverage of 117 companies and that it will eventually cover more companies with fewer analysts.

How It Breaks Down

The bulge bracket. There's no clear and uniformly accepted definition of this group, but it basically includes the biggest of the full-service investment banks. This is the group that matters most in investment banking, and their names confer distinction, whether you're a start-up with an IPO to sell, a *Fortune* 500 company planning an acquisition, or a job seeker sending out resumes. Merrill Lynch, Morgan Stanley, Goldman Sachs, Citigroup, Lehman Brothers, Credit Suisse First Boston, Deutsche Bank, and J.P. Morgan Chase hold top spots in this bracket, at least for the moment. A whole host of others fall into the second tier of major players, including Bear Stearns and UBS Warburg, the investment-banking division of the giant Swiss bank, UBS.

Boutiques and regional firms. Obviously, the investment banking world extends beyond New York and the bulge bracket, but the list of small firms is getting smaller as the market consolidates. The strongest boutique firms—Hambrecht & Quist, Montgomery Securities, and Alex. Brown—have all been acquired by commercial banks. But that's not to say independent firms are nearing extinction. The equity markets are strong, and that means big business for niche firms focusing on technology, biotechnology, and other high-growth industries. In New York, Allen & Co. and Lazard Frères still do big business in specialized fields. Volpe Brown Whelan and Thomas Weisel are Silicon Valley firms capitalizing on their technology connections and expertise.

Key Jobs for MBAs

Jobs in investment banks are divided into four areas: corporate finance, sales, trading, and research. Movement between areas isn't unheard of, but since doing your time and moving up the ranks in one area is the quickest way to make a lot of money, most people stay put.

Corporate finance. Think of corporate finance as financial consulting to businesses. Specific activities range from underwriting the sale of equity or debt for a corporate client to providing advice on mergers and acquisitions, foreign exchange, economic and market trends, and specific financial strategies. When most people refer to investment banking, this is what they mean.

CorpFin (as it is known internally) analysts work 80-hour weeks to help prepare (i.e., proofread and Xerox) pitch books to compete against other banks for prospective clients. They run endless financial models and help prepare (again, proofread and Xerox) due diligence on target companies. After two or three years, they're bustled off to B-school.

MBAs are brought in at the associate level, where they help underwrite equity (stocks) and fixed-income (bond) offerings, write sections of pitch books, and sit in on client meetings—mostly taking notes—and help devise financial strategies. They also supervise teams of analysts. After three or four years, they move up to vice president; after another three to five years, they make it to managing director.

Salary range: $100,000 to $170,000, including bonuses, for associates, and $200,000 to $300,000 or more, including bonuses, for VPs.

Sales. Some firms only hire MBAs for sales jobs. Other firms don't even ask about your education. In either case, the bottom line is how well you can sell the new debt and equity issues CorpFin unloads on your desk—and how quickly you can translate news events or a market shift into transactions for your clients. These jobs are usually much less hierarchical than the banking side. Your sales volume and asset growth are what matter.

Salary range: MBAs start at $70,000 to $85,000, with a signing bonus of up to $20,000. Year-end bonuses fluctuate; they can be as high as 80 to 100 percent of base pay.

Trading. When Hollywood directors want to portray the rough, unruly underside of Wall Street, they wheel the cameras onto a trading floor. This is as close to the money as you can get. Trading also commands respect because it's tougher, riskier, and more intense than any other job in finance. Traders manage the firm's risk and make markets by setting the prices—based on supply and demand—for the securities CorpFin has underwritten. Like sales, but more so, you're tied to your desk and phones while the markets are open— but you get to leave after the closing bell.

Beginners fetch endless take-out food and run other thankless errands; more seasoned traders scream and yell when their markets heat up and do the crossword puzzle the rest of the time. Not for the genteel or the faint of heart. A few traders even grow up to be CEOs. Why? Because they know more about the markets and money than anyone else in banking.

Salary range: Similar to that in sales.

Research analyst. Research departments are generally divided into fixed income (debt) and equity. Both do quantitative research (corporate-financing strategies, product development, and pricing models), economic research (forecasts for U.S. and international markets, interest rates, currencies), and individual company coverage. An equity analyst usually focuses on a particular sector— software, oil and gas, or health care, for example.

You move up in this profession by consistently predicting the movement of specific company stocks. The best analysts are ranked annually by Institutional Investor magazine. Their buy, sell, and hold recommendations wield enormous clout, and competition among firms for the top analysts can be intense.

Salary range: For the few undergrads and MBAs hired, starting salaries and signing bonuses are often slightly higher than the rest of investment banking. Senior analysts earn six figures and up (way up). Their bonuses and periodic raises are closely tied to the accuracy of their quarterly earnings projections.

Key Investment Banks by 2002 Revenue

Company	Revenue ($M)	% Change from 2001	# of Employees
J.P. Morgan Chase	43,372	−14	94,335
Morgan Stanley	32,415	−26	55,726
Deutsche Bank	31,238	−53	77,442
Merrill Lynch	28,253	−27	50,900
Goldman Sachs Group	22,854	−27	19,739
Citigroup	21,250	−22	40,000
Lehman Brothers	16,781	−25	12,343
UBS Warburg	12,760*	5*	15,964
Credit Lyonnais	8,084	2	41,349*
Nomura Holdings	9,962	−3	15,000
Bear Stearns	6,891	−21	10,574
Credit Suisse First Boston USA	5,739	−24	11,565
AG Edwards	2,364	−17	16,700

*2001 figures. Sources: Hoovers.com; WetFeet analysis.

Additional Resources

Hoover's Financial Services Industry Snapshot
(http://www.hoovers.com/industry/snapshot/profile/0,3519,18,00.html)

Institutional Investor Online (http://www.institutionalinvestor.com)

Investors' Business Daily (http://www.investors.com)

Knowledge @ Wharton: Finance and Investment
(http://knowledge.wharton.upenn.edu/category.cfm?catid=1)

McKinsey Quarterly: Financial Services
(http://www.mckinseyquarterly.com/category_editor.asp?L2=10)

McKinsey Quarterly: Corporate Finance
(http://www.mckinseyquarterly.com/category_editor.asp?L2=5)

Ohio State University List of Finance Sites
(http://www.cob.ohio-state.edu/fin/journal/jofsites.htm)

Mutual Funds & Brokerage

Industry Overview

When a large amount of money is needed for any enterprise, from building a factory to funding a corporation to drilling wells in a new oil field, that money is raised from investors—usually a large number of them. Commonly, the enterprise raises that money by either selling ownership shares in itself or simply borrowing it. When ownership is sold, the investor gets stock shares. When money is borrowed, the investor gets bonds. Stocks and bonds are both securities. Investors buy and sell individual securities through brokers, also called securities dealers.

Additionally, mutual fund companies—and other so-called asset management firms—form funds, which consist of a variety of securities. The asset management company buys and sells the securities in a fund, seeking to maximize its value, and it sells shares in these funds to investors directly and through securities brokers. The mutual fund company charges a fee for picking the securities in a fund. In turn, the shareholder is shielded from the risk of investing in individual securities.

But why lump together two previously distinct areas of the financial services industry—securities brokerage and asset management? Principally because the way your parents invested is not how most people do it these days. More people invest in securities today than ever before, and they have more choices. Not only are there more investments to choose from, including stocks, bonds, real-estate trusts, limited partnerships, and an ever-growing diversity of mutual funds; there are also more ways to invest: full-service brokerages, discount

brokerages, and electronic trading for most of us; exclusive opportunities such as hedge funds and venture capital funds for so-called high net-worth individuals, such as multimillionaires, and institutional investors, such as pension funds, insurance companies, and university endowments.

There is an unimaginably large amount of money chasing investments these days, which is part of the reason that the stock market rose so steeply during the 1990s. Brokerages and mutual funds are the two primary means by which all these investments are made.

Trends

The financial supermarket. Brokerage firms (e.g., Merrill Lynch, Citigroup, and discounters Charles Schwab and E-Trade) and mutual funds (e.g., Fidelity, Vanguard, and Dreyfus) have invaded each other's turf in an ever-escalating financial-services war. Fidelity was the first fund to offer a large discount-brokerage operation. Virtually every national and regional brokerage firm now offers its own family of mutual funds, in addition to traditional offerings of funds run by other firms like Fidelity, Eaton Vance, Nuveen, Putnam, and MFS. But all that was merely prelude.

In late 1999, Congress repealed the 1933 Glass-Steagall Act, opening the door for banks, securities brokers, and insurance companies to engage in each other's formerly exclusive businesses, without restrictions. More consolidation of financial companies and of services within individual companies has followed. The aisles of financial supermarkets of the future will be lined with not just mutual funds, but every other kind of brokered investment—even credit transactions. In one account you might combine mutual funds; individual stocks, bonds, and options; credit products such as credit cards, credit lines, and home mortgages; and even a money market checking account.

Fearful investors. The struggling economy, an increasing number of examples of corporate financial shenanigans, and a plummeting stock market have combined to give investors cold feet-quite a change from the late 1990s, when everyone from the guy behind the counter at the corner deli to your neighborhood pedicurist was talking about corporate earnings and upcoming stock splits and looking forward to tearing open the envelope containing their next brokerage-account statement. Nowadays, individual investors are staying away from the market. Which means fewer trades and fewer commission dollars for brokers, and less money going into mutual funds, and thus lower commission revenues for them as well. Unless the market turns around, the corporate-accounting scandals dry up and blow away, or the Bush administration starts doing a better job of reassuring investors about U.S. business prospects, it appears the new paradigm of softer investment-services earnings will be around for a while. Which is not good news for job seekers.

How It Breaks Down

Though we divide the industry up into brokerages and mutual funds, within the two segments there are significant differences among the players. You'll want to make sure you not only know which segment you're interested in, but also how the particular company with which you're interviewing is distinguished from the competition.

Brokerage. A broker acts as the intermediary between the buyer and seller in a securities transaction. The buyer and seller, not the brokerage firm, assume the risk. (If the firm acts as the principal or dealer, it deals from its own account and assumes some of the risk itself.) Brokers charge their clients a commission. A full-service firm such as Merrill Lynch charges commissions up to several hundreds of dollars for transactions but offers extras such as tailored research,

strategy and planning, and asset-management accounts—checking, credit (including lending on margin), and brokerage, all in one convenient package.

A discount broker, such as TD Waterhouse, generally just executes trade orders and issues a confirmation—few or no frills. Frills or no frills, to be authorized to trade on the various exchanges you need to be a registered representative and licensed by the NASD (National Association of Securities Dealers).

Mutual funds. Whereas brokers act on investors' orders, mutual-fund managers raise cash from shareholders and then invest it in stocks, bonds, money-market securities, currencies, options, gold, or whatever else seems likely to make money. Mutual funds often have a specific investment focus—be it income, long-term growth, small cap, large cap, or foreign companies. And managers are restricted in what kinds of investments they can make. Compared to individual portfolios, funds hope to persuade investors they offer several advantages: professional money management; liquidity; and more diversification than most individuals can create or afford in a personal portfolio, particularly now that switching between funds is allowed.

All investors share equally in the gains and losses of a fund, and probably the most important factor in choosing one—whether to work for or invest in—is your tolerance for risk. Bull markets tend to make many funds look good, but a downward turn or a jump in interest rates can have a significant negative impact that may take longer to correct for a fund than in the nimble independent investor's portfolio.

Key Jobs for MBAs

Portfolio manager (mutual funds). Portfolio fund managers use their knowledge of investment theory, market experience, research from staff and outside companies, and occasionally plain dumb luck to pick investments for their fund portfolios. Then if the fund outperforms the relevant market indices, the money floods in. If not, the tide pulls the other way. To reach the pinnacle in this profession, count on many years in the ranks of investment advisory and money management. Insiders also point out that passing the SEC's Series 7 exam is necessary in order to be registered and that the Chartered Financial Analyst (CFA) designation is a huge plus for people planning on entering portfolio management.

Salary range: $70,000 to $500,000, with a handful earning more than $1 million.

Wholesaler. Brokers and many of their clients tend to like passive investments, and funds are ideal for these types of people. But they may also want a little more involvement in fund information and more details than Mr. and Mrs. J.Q. Public. Enter the wholesaler from mutual fund XYZ, ready to host a "client appreciation program." Wholesalers market their funds to huge clients such as Merrill and Morgan Stanley, but also must focus on smaller brokers and independent financial advisors. This is nice work if you can get it, and most wholesalers do well.

Salary range: $75,000 to $200,000 or $300,000, with liberal expense accounts for meals and seminars.

Analyst or researcher. Here you delve into the "fundamentals," examining every single feature of a security to determine if it's really a buy. You specialize in a certain industry or an industry segment and come to know the companies that compete there inside out. Expect to give computer screens lots of quality time and to really get cozy with annual reports. If you don't like reading, accounting, crunching numbers, and more reading, you won't be happy here. But it's excellent training for more substantive and lucrative investment-advisory work or portfolio management. Top MBAs sometimes land plum industry assignments; everyone else has to cover trucking and footwear for a while before moving up to telecommunications, technology, and financial services.

Salary range: $50,000 to $100,000, plus bonuses of like amounts or more.

Financial planner. How is a one-income family going to pay for its kids' college education? How soon, if ever, can a graphic artist retire? Financial planners help people work out these and other difficult money problems. In some ways, this is a thankless job. Even wealthy people don't much enjoy tackling these issues head on, and everyone else actively dreads it. But if you sympathize with that anxiety and know a lot about tax law and different investment strategies, you can do quite well in this business. You can also do it alone with a fair amount of flexibility. Whether you decide to be independent or join a firm, many of these professionals now opt for a CFP (Certified Financial Planner) certification.

Salary range: $60,000 to $120,000. The very best can earn more than $250,000, typically working on a fee or commission basis.

Sales and marketing. These jobs are similar to product management positions at consumer products companies, but the products are financial products. People in sales no longer focus on fund or investment. They need to be able to sell any one of a growing spectrum of financial products, depending on a

customer's short- and long-term needs—and whatever his brother-in-law told him to do last week. This is forecast as one of the strongest areas for jobs in the next five to ten years. Marketers focus on both the long-term picture and specific current product offerings. Who needs what and how much will they pay for it?

Salary range: $40,000 to $100,000, not including bonuses, which can range into six figures.

Key Mutual Funds and Brokerage Firms by 2002 Revenue

Company	Revenue ($M)	% Change from 2001	# of Employees
J.P. Morgan Chase	43,372	−14	94,335
Morgan Stanley	32,415	-26	55,726
Merrill Lynch	28,253	-27	50,900
FMR Corp.	8,900	-9	29,000
Mellon Financial	4,737	17	22,500
Alliance Capital Mgmt	2,742	-8	4,172
Franklin Resources	2,519	7	6,700
A.G. Edwards	2,364	-17	16,700
Amvescap	2,168	-8	8,519*
Putnam	2,166	-17	5,600
Legg Mason	1,615	2	5,290
Vanguard Group	1,568	-8	10,000
Janus Capital Group	1,145	-26	1,450
T. Rowe Price Group	918	-11	3,710
Schroders	788	7	2,890*
Federated Investors	706	0	1,706

*2001 figures. Sources: Hoovers.com; WetFeet analysis.

Additional Resources

Association for Investment Management and Research (AIMR)
(http://www.aimr.org)

Financial Analysts Journal (http://www.aimrpubs.org/faj/home.html)

Institutional Investor Online (http://www.institutionalinvestor.com)

Investors' Business Daily (http://www.investors.com)

Knowledge @ Wharton: Finance and Investment
(http://knowledge.wharton.upenn.edu/category.cfm?catid=1)

McKinsey Quarterly: Financial Services
(http://www.mckinseyquarterly.com/category_editor.asp?L2=10)

Ohio State University List of Finance Sites
(http://www.cob.ohio-state.edu/fin/journal/jofsites.htm)

Networking & Peripherals

Industry Overview

We are all connected to each other. Today, we're wired into the telephone grid, but we're about to be linked in many other ways, probably sooner than we think. Computer peripherals and networks are both playing a huge role in the new ways we connect. What exactly does this industry encompass? One insider describes it as "whatever you plug into the box, internally or externally: the modems, monitors, printers, scanners, Iomega Zip drives, microphones, speakers, video graphic cards, plus the networks—all the spaghetti that connects all of the various boxes together."

Peripherals and networks each serve two very different markets, and job seekers need to be aware of the distinction. One, the consumer and small-business market, buys peripherals, such as printers, removable storage drives, mice, modems, monitors, and, increasingly, low-end network devices, scanners, and digital audio and imaging peripherals. Major vendors here include Epson, Logitech, HP, Iomega, Canon, and Sony. The second, a much more sophisticated market, is the high-end professional and corporate market. Peripherals for these buyers include high-performance, network-ready laser and color printers; backup and RAID storage; production-quality scanners; and other specialized audio and graphics accessories. Networks for the most part still focus on exacting IT customers in the business markets. The big names in networking include Cisco, 3Com, and Lucent.

This industry does most of its manufacturing outside the United States, in places like Taiwan, Singapore, and Ireland. Some factories are owned and run

by the companies who sell their products, but a lot of the manufacturing is done by so-called original equipment manufacturers (OEMs), who act as suppliers, often under license, to big-name manufacturers. The contribution of the OEM varies. A manufacturer may add a lot of its own technology to a major component from an OEM. For example, HP gets the imaging engines of its laser printers from Canon, but HP adds its own electronics before putting its name on the box. Or a marketing company may not add anything except its brand to a CD-ROM drive or modem manufactured by an OEM.

While U.S. firms largely do their manufacturing elsewhere, they do most of their design and marketing here. And U.S. employees also manage offshore factories owned by their firms. So if you are interested in engineering or sales and marketing, there are jobs in this industry for you. There are also jobs in finance, IT, and management, including overseas jobs in those offshore factories. Finally, as in other high-tech industries, jobs exist in communications and graphic arts, from technical writing to marketing communications (marcom).

Trends

Convergence. The 1996 Telecommunications Act marked the official start of a digital land rush. New competitors—publishers, television networks, telecoms, and cable television companies—are dashing to stake claims for virtual territory in cyberspace. The buzzword used to describe this is convergence, meaning that content-the industry's term for information-will be delivered electronically through phone lines, cable, satellites, or cellular connections (take your choice). You will view it on your computer, high-definition television, or wireless phone (choose all that apply). It will be paid for by advertising, subscription, or cybercash (nobody knows).

Despite the uncertainties, a lot of very big companies are betting that some version of this will happen, and they are blurring the lines between networks and computers. "Think of it as a telephone," says one systems developer. "You can have pretty much any size or shape or color you want, and it can have lots of extra features or none. But the real point of the phone—or the next-generation computer—is the external connection, not its individual characteristics."

Poor financial performance. This industry has been hit harder by recent events than many others. Dot coms, with their networking needs, were a major revenue driver for networking companies. So, with the dot-com sector dead in the water, a major source of networking sales has all but disappeared. Telecom companies were another big revenue driver, but with the current telecom infrastructure over capacity, there's less demand from that sector as well. Add to all this the fact that companies of all stripes are cutting costs, and you get a very weak market. Even the mighty Cisco is suffering from poor financial performance-revenue in the second quarter of 2002 was down for the second year in a row-and poor stock-price performance.

Bright spot: handhelds and gaming consoles. Companies like Palm and other PDA makers are among the few in the industry that are enjoying growth. Led by the growth in usage of wireless e-mail, this sector saw sales growth of about 25 percent in 2002. And with the growth in the gaming sector, Nintendo, Sony, and Microsoft are hoping to make a hefty chunk of change on consoles.

How It Breaks Down

This is a difficult industry to segment. It serves a wide spectrum of markets—from the high school Web surfer to the CIO implementing a million-dollar enterprise-wide e-commerce system—each with different needs and buying habits. It produces an enormous variety of products—from digital cameras and

printers to network hubs and joysticks. And this industry distributes its products through many channels: value-added resellers, systems integrators, consultants, direct sales, and even several varieties of retail. So we'll just describe the major product categories. Jobs abound in all these categories, although some categories are growing faster than others. All are subject to periodic layoffs, a reflection of the underlying volatility of high-tech industries in general. But all are also subject to periodic booms, when companies can't hire people fast enough, especially those with technical skills. And all do the vast majority of their manufacturing outside the United States.

Add-in cards. These include sound cards, LAN cards, video cards, and graphics cards, among others. Previously marketed as after-market add-ons, these increasingly come built into new PCs, either as cards or as functionality built onto the motherboard. As computer prices have fallen, the predominant trend for most consumers now is to buy a new computer rather than two new peripherals. In fact, manufacturers are pushing the idea of stripped down, inexpensive computers with all functionality on the motherboard and no slots for add-on cards at all.

Input/output peripherals. These include any device that lets data enter or exit a computer-from necessities such as monitors and keyboards to task-specific items such as joysticks, scanners, printers, or optical disk jukeboxes. Thousands of companies—including many in Japan and elsewhere in Asia—manufacture peripherals for the consumer or business markets, or both.

Storage peripherals. The capacities of storage devices keep growing, as users increasingly create and share documents that contain graphics, video, and sound components requiring large amounts of disk space. Astoundingly, the price of a gigabyte of storage continues to drop dramatically. Today, companies generally

produce and share a far greater volume of documents than they used to, and they need even more powerful backup drives for protection and storage. Iomega's 100-meg Zip drive, which a few years ago seemed immense, is now common for many home users. Recordable CDs are increasingly used for archival purposes.

Again, where you look for work in this area depends on whether you opt for the consumer or the high-end and corporate market. IBM, Iomega, Quantum, Seagate, Maxtor, and Western Digital are useful starting points if this sector interests you. A large number of companies produce storage systems consisting of drives to which they add specialized electronics, software, ruggedization (in which components are modified to withstand unusually harsh operating conditions in military or industrial applications) or other added value.

Network equipment. Networking and connectivity hardware are among the most dynamic areas for job seekers right now, certainly more so than most peripherals. And the ultimate integration of print, broadcast, and other media into the converged, digital data stream will make networks that much more important. Amazingly, only a few years ago AT&T and IBM were the undisputed kingpins here; no one could imagine a Lucent, 3Com, or Cisco controlling even a portion of the network.

Key Jobs for MBAs

Product manager. As a product manager, you're a key player in coming up with product ideas and working with engineers to make them a reality. This position requires some grasp of technical matters, the ability to build consensus and teamwork (translation: If you're not good at office politics, don't raise your hand for this one), and a knack for spotting and anticipating market trends.

Salary range: $50,000 to $80,000.

Financial analyst. Financial analysis in computer hardware companies can take many forms: numerical analysis for production planning, industrial operations management, and general finance and accounting. In some cases, analysts evaluate other companies as potential merger or acquisition targets. These are expanding divisions in most of the larger companies right now and a good way to learn about the industry overall before you settle on a particular focus.

Salary range: $50,000 to $70,000.

Key Networking & Peripherals Manufacturers by 2002 Revenue			
Company	Revenue ($M)	% Change from 2001	# of Employees
IBM	81,186	-6	355,421
HP	56,588	25	141,00
Cisco	18,915	-15	36,000
Xerox	15,849	-7	67,800
Sun Microsystems	12,495	-32	39,400
Lucent	12,321	-42	47,000
Nortel Networks	10,560	-40	36,960
Canon USA	8,418	13	11,000
3Com	1,478	-48	4,615
Juniper Networks	547	-38	1,542
Source: Hoovers.com; WetFeet analysis.			

Additional Resources

CrossNodes (http://networking.earthweb.com)

HardwareCentral (http://hardware.earthweb.com)

Hoover's Computer Hardware Industry Snapshot
(http://www.hoovers.com/industry/snapshot/profile/0,3519,12,00.html)

Nonprofit & Government

Industry Overview

Some 20 million people work for government-agencies and departments that on a federal, state, or local level handle issues as diverse as highway construction and the protection of wilderness areas, public health programs and subsidies to tobacco farmers, the space program and fireworks displays on the Fourth of July. Governments collect taxes and use them to fund programs. That includes everything from a small-town government filling potholes on Main Street, to a big city providing police and fire fighting services, to a state issuing drivers licenses, to the federal government sending troops into combat, or making Medicare payments to a long-term health care facility for the elderly poor.

Federal and state legislators make laws, and city and county supervisors pass ordinances. Executive agencies-from the White House to the state house to city hall-issue regulations. Governments employ armies of civil servants, bureaucrats, lawyers, and specialists of all kinds to implement their policies and staff their programs. These include people who analyze policy and draft legislation for U.S. Senators, people who issue building permits at town hall, and everyone in between.

Even though most employees in this sector enjoy excellent benefits, there can be downsides to working in government. For one thing, the pay is often lower in these positions than in their private-sector equivalents. And in many government positions, jobs are politicized: Your priorities can change with the election cycle, and the program you're working on or the representative you work for may not even be around next year.

Nonprofit organizations are businesses designed to make change, and not in the monetary sense. Granted 501(c)3, or tax-exempt, status by the government, these organizations focus on a wide variety of causes, including everything from the Africa Fund, which promotes human rights, education, and people-to-people exchanges with African countries, to the National Breast Cancer Foundation. Many nonprofit interest groups, such as the Clean Water Fund and the Center on Budget and Policy Priorities, are located in Washington, D.C., where they lobby government on behalf of their causes. Others have offices near state legislatures, lobbying here too for the passage of legislation favorable to their causes.

Nonprofits derive their operating revenues from foundations, government grants, membership dues, and fees for services they provide. Nonprofits typically attract people passionate about solving social problems; the big upside of working in this sector is that you can make a positive impact on behalf of your organization's cause. The downside is that most jobs in the nonprofit sector, like many in the government sector, don't pay very well.

Trends

Social enterprise. One of the reasons nonprofits don't pay so well is that funding sources are increasingly scarce. As the government cuts budgets, there's a greater need for the services provided by nonprofits—but at the same time, there's less government funding available for them. As a result, many nonprofits have sought new ways to get cash. In particular, they've begun looking at the private sector to learn how to operate more efficiently; some have even spun off businesses to help raise money and create jobs. For instance, Seattle-based Pioneer Human Services, which provides a variety of services to the socially

disadvantaged, has developed a number of business enterprises, including a real estate division and a metal factory. Delancey Street Foundation in San Francisco was one of the first philanthropic organizations to combine for-profit ventures with social consciousness: Its moneymaking enterprises are staffed primarily by recovering drug addicts.

New terms have entered currency to describe this harnessing of entrepreneurial business acumen by nonprofit causes: venture philanthropy, social entrepreneurism, and social return on investment (SROI). The nonprofit sector is still an area for people who want to make a difference in the world, but more so than ever, that goal requires money, experience, and education as well as genuine dedication.

Technology and the government. At first, the Internet was just another newfangled piece of technology that the government had to worry about regulating. Then politicians realized, "Hey, I can ceaselessly blather to an ungodly number of people, and it's free!" Technology is seeping into the government sector: chat online with the President, e-mail your congressman, or peruse the Library of Congress from your living room. Thomas Jefferson would have thought it was cool.

Nonprofit is hot. Nonprofits are among the most desirable places to work for many job seekers these days. Whether it's because of the demise of the dot coms, the spate of layoffs in technology, or the terrorist attacks of September 11, 2001, people seem to have changed their career focus from getting rich quick to doing something meaningful for themselves and for society. This is good news for nonprofits, which are getting a larger pool of talented candidates to choose from, but not the best news for job seekers. Still, those with a real interest in nonprofit should be able to find a good fit somewhere in this sector, especially if they have experience in the field.

How It Breaks Down

Nonprofits. There are a number of ways to break down the nonprofit sector. For instance, nonprofits can be divided into those that focus on lobbying government on behalf of a cause (interest groups, such as the National Rifle Association) and those that focus on providing services to society (such as museums or homes for pregnant teens). But the best way to break down this sector is probably by cause.

To get a sense of the variety of nonprofits, here's a short list of causes and the organizations that serve them: arts and education (Friends of the Library, the Washington Ballet, the New York Philharmonic, the Boy Scouts, the Girl Scouts, 4H, the National Center on Family Literacy), civil and human rights (Amnesty International, the American Civil Liberties Union, the National Immigration Forum, the NAACP, Planned Parenthood), the environment (the Environmental Defense Fund, the National Wildlife Federation, the Nature Conservancy, the Sierra Club), and economic and social justice (the American Association of Retired Persons, the Center for the Child Care Workforce, the National Low Income Housing Coalition, the Salvation Army, the United Way).

Alongside the large national and international nonprofits are myriad locally based, smaller nonprofits; like their bigger cousins, these break down by mission and include everything from community theater troupes to women's shelters to convalescent homes.

Capitol Hill and Federal Government. The executive branch agencies comprise the largest group of federal government jobs, including the Social Security Administration, the Environmental Protection Agency, the FBI, the National Endowment for the Humanities, the Bureau of Indian Affairs, and the Bureau of Engraving and Printing. (There are also jobs available in agencies under the

aegis of the judicial and legislative branches, such as in the Library of Congress or the Congressional Budget Office.) There are two basic types of positions in the various government agencies: civil service positions and political appointments (also called Schedule C appointments).

Not all people with federal agency jobs are based in Washington, D.C. Think of all those postal employees out on the streets of America, braving rain, sleet, and snow. Or the diplomat at the U.S. embassy in Cairo. Or the park ranger in Yellowstone National Park. Think of the bureaucrats in federal office buildings in every major U.S. city, the Bureau of Indian Affairs agent on some isolated reservation in New Mexico, the civilian technician maintaining communications gear in the tropical heat of Guam, the medical researcher culturing bacteria at the Centers for Disease Control in Atlanta.

Congressional jobs, on the other hand, are more concentrated geographically. Congress—the legislative branch—is divided into the House, which consists of one representative from each of 435 districts in the country (and several nonvoting delegates), and the Senate, which is made up of 100 senators, two from each state. Most people who work for the legislative branch of the federal government are based in Washington, D.C. They are on the staffs of legislators or legislative agencies, such as the Library of Congress or the Congressional Office of the Budget. Congresspeople and senators also maintain staffs in their home districts and states. Every senator and representative hires a staff to assist with his or her job, and this is where many opportunities exist in Washington for young people, provided they have good educations and, usually, good connections.

Like the federal government, state governments consist of various executive-branch agencies along with a legislative body, all of which offer opportunities to job seekers. Similarly, local governments, including those of townships,

counties, and cities, offer a range of political and agency job opportunities; consider public health, community development, and court administration.

Nongovernment political jobs. In addition to the job opportunities that exist within government, there are plenty of political opportunities that technically are not within government. For example, many people work at lobbying firms (including Patton, Boggs & Blow; Akin, Gump, Strauss, Hauer & Feld; and Verner, Liipfert, Bernhard, McPherson & Hand), nonprofit interest groups (like the American Medical Association or the Teamsters Union), and think tanks (such as the Brookings Institute, the Heritage Foundation, and the Cato Institute). Most of these organizations are located in Washington, D.C., and in the various state capitals. Both the Democratic and the Republican parties have national committees as well as state and local offices where job seekers interested in working for a political party may find opportunities.

Key Jobs for MBAs

Program director. In larger nonprofits and a handful of small ones, a tier of mid-level management is needed. Duties include oversight and management of a specific program, often including hiring personnel, fund-raising, public relations, and all other administrative and management duties specific to the program area. The program director usually reports directly to the executive director.

Salary range: $35,000 to $70,000.

Executive director. The grand pooh-bah of the nonprofit organization, the executive director is the equivalent of a CEO and reports directly to the board of directors. He or she is financially accountable for the organization and oversees all strategic planning and management. Depending on the size of the

nonprofit, the executive director may be involved with other duties as well, including fund-raising and development, board development, hiring of personnel, media relations, program development, and just about anything else that needs to be done.

Salary range: $75,000 and up.

Project manager. Government project managers work in regulatory agencies, where they manage the process of regulatory review through all its stages. (Think of IRS agents auditing a business or SEC officials investigating charges against a brokerage house.) The job typically requires experience in the regulated industry, an MBA, or equivalent skills.

Salary range: $48,000 to $75,000.

📁 Key Nonprofits in 2002	
Organization	**Operating Income ($B)**
Lutheran Industries in America	7.65
National Council of YMCAs	4.12
American Red Cross	2.71
Catholic Charities USA	2.62
United Jewish Communities	2.23
Goodwill Industries	1.94
Salvation Army	1.91
Fidelity Investment Charitable Gift Fund	1.25
Boys & Girls Club of America	1.00
American Cancer Society	0.92
Source: *The NonProfit Times.*	

Key U.S. Govt. Agencies by Number of Civilian Employees, 2001		
Agency/Department	Federal Budget Outlay (est. $B)	# of Civilian Employees
U.S. Postal Service	n/a	847,821
Defense	294.0	671,591
Veterans' Affairs	45.8	225,893
Treasury	390.6	148,186
Justice	21.3	127,783
Agriculture	68.6	108,540
Interior	8.2	75,846
Transportation	54.8	65,542
Social Security Administration	462.0	65,351
Health & Human Services	426.8	64,343

Sources: 2002 U.S. Statistical Abstract (U.S. Census Bureau); WetFeet analysis.

Additional Resources

Careers in Government (http://www.careersingovernment.com)

McKinsey Quarterly: Nonprofit
(http://www.mckinseyquarterly.com/category_editor.asp?L2=33)

Nonprofit Career Network (http://www.nonprofitcareer.com)

The Chronicle of Philanthropy (http://philanthropy.com)

The Foundation Center (http://fdncenter.org)

The NonProfit Times (http://www.nptimes.com)

The U.S. Government Manual
(http://www.access.gpo.gov/nara/browse-gm-01.html)

Real Estate

Industry Overview

The real estate industry's pared-down definition is land. However, it's much more complicated than that. The industry involves the buying, selling, renting, leasing, and management of commercial, residential, agricultural, and other kinds of property, including all the functions that support such activity, such as appraising and financing. The successful realtor is necessarily a shrewd salesperson with a deep knowledge of real estate markets and a broad understanding of the contracts, laws, and tax regulations that apply to real estate transactions.

The industry is a cyclical one, with booms and busts tied closely to the economy's overall performance. With corporations facing difficult times and more people unemployed, commercial real estate is experiencing major weakness. Rents have fallen all over the place after the bubble of the 1990s, and in cities with a concentration of tech-related companies, vacancy rates are skyrocketing. For example, commercial vacancy rates in San Francisco, Denver, and Seattle exceeded 30 percent in 2002.

In spite of the ups and downs, real estate is the source of almost half the privately owned wealth in the United States. It is an industry famous for making people filthy rich and is responsible for more than five million jobs in the United States. Thinking big is part of the real estate industry, and grandiose speculation has created some of America's greatest fortunes. John Jacob Astor traded in his empire of beaver pelts for a gamble on uptown Manhattan real estate and in the process became the richest man in America. More recently,

moguls like Sam "the grave dancer" Zell and the perennially overreaching Donald Trump have made fantastic fortunes on real estate gambles. Even for non-billionaires in the industry, the thrill of deal making, the potential for financial reward, and the sociability make real estate a rewarding profession.

Trends

Restructuring. Real estate has been undergoing a major restructuring. Aggressive consolidation and a wave of strategic alliances have resulted in two tiers of players in the industry. At the top are large multi-service firms, such as Trammell Crow and Lasalle Partners, with enough capital and resources to withstand economic downturns. The bottom tier includes smaller developers and agencies that are more flexible and better able to service local markets. Meanwhile, midlevel operators are getting pushed out. For job seekers, this means you are most likely to work for either a local or a national firm.

REITs. Real estate investment trusts (REITs), developed over the past decade or so, pool money from many investors and invest it in an array of properties. With access to massive amounts of capital, they can buy, develop, and speculate in large properties. Two of the largest owners of office and residential property in the United States, Equity Office Properties Trust and Equity Residential Properties Trust, are REITs.

Residential real estate looking solid—for now. Home prices have been surprisingly solid despite the economic downturn. Even in cities such as San Francisco where rents have dropped, the residential market has weakened but remains relatively strong. Companies like Pulte have found that while demand has softened at the top of the market, it remains strong for lower-end homes. But some warn that this is yet another bubble market—that the gap between

rents and house-purchase prices suggests that people are buying homes they can't really afford, and that the bottom may drop out on residential real estate. In any case, if the economic downturn continues for very long, and consumer confidence falls, residential real estate is certain to soften moving forward.

How It Breaks Down

Job opportunities in the industry are divided into four distinct fields: sales, management, development, and acquisition and analysis. Although crossover among these sectors is possible, most people start out specializing in a specific area.

Sales and leasing. This segment includes everything from residential real estate brokers such as Century 21 and Coldwell Banker to larger corporations that broker bigger commercial properties such as office towers. Grubb & Ellis has one of the largest global brokerage divisions, offering sales and leasing services in many U.S. markets and in Europe. Cushman & Wakefield is another giant, with offices nationwide. Its clients are primarily corporations and other institutions, for which it negotiates sales and leases.

Management. Property managers are responsible for maintaining property values. They deal with tenants, manage finances, and physically tend to the property. Of all the segments of the industry, this one has been hit hardest by the wave of mergers and acquisitions sweeping the industry. Some industry insiders are predicting that 75 percent of the property management firms in operation in 1990 will be out of business by the year 2007. For job seekers, this means fewer jobs as companies look to become more efficient and cut redundant staff.

Development. Developers are responsible for taking a property idea and making it a reality. This is a complex process involving architects, engineers, zoning officials, builders, lenders, and prospective tenants. Development is not always the gravy train some make it out to be. In the early 1990s, when real estate prices crashed, construction dried up and a lot of commercial office space was left vacant. Deprived of rents, a lot of developers had to scramble for survival. Many ventured into other areas of real estate. Today, many of the largest real estate developers are also property owners and managers.

Acquisition and analysis. Any kind of investing in real estate requires a thorough understanding of how to analyze the value of a property and navigate the maze of land-use regulations, zoning laws, environmental impact reports, financing realities, and other barriers to buying and developing a property. The people who develop, market, and manage REITs and other real estate investments are financial types, often MBAs, who are charged with evaluating and arranging for the purchase of properties.

Key Jobs for MBAs

The great thing about real estate is it's not going away. It's the level of demand and how many jobs the market can support that will fluctuate. For salespeople, there's plenty of competition. On the management side, there is the popularity of rental housing and a rising number of job opportunities in apartment and assisted-living management. Those who want security can find work as appraisers, as these jobs are less affected by the industry cycle.

Consultant or advisor. With the increase in institutional investing, demand for this type of expert has risen. Prior experience in investing or management is necessary. A real estate advisor is generally good with statistics and excels at dealing with clients.

Salary range: $50,000 and up.

Developer. A developer makes property plans come to life. To become a developer, you'll need excellent communication skills and a strong understanding of all aspects of the real estate industry. Most developers start out in entry-level positions with a developer or contractor and then work their way up.

Salary range: $50,000 to $100,000 or more.

Entrepreneur. A real estate entrepreneur buys property for the purpose of making money. Success as an entrepreneur takes an equal mix of industry smarts and good fortune. Just remember that although many people have made fortunes in real estate, even more haven't.

Salary range: The sky's the limit, but the threat of bankruptcy is very real.

Key Real Estate Companies by 2002 Revenue

Company	Revenue ($M)	% Change from 2001	# of Employees
Cendant Corp.	14,088	59	85,000
Centex Corp.	9,117	18	16,249
The Trump Org.	8,500	0	22,000
Pulte Homes	7,472	39	9,200
Lennar Corp.	7,320	21	9,419
KB Home	4,939	10	4,500
Starwood Hotels & Resorts	4,659	17	105,000
The LeFrak Org.*	3,800	19	16,200
Host Marriott	3,696	-3	189
Equity Office Properties Trust	3,613	10	2,500
NRT	3,159	13	52,801
The Ryland Group	2,877	5	2,458
Hilton Hotels Corp.	2,540	-4	74,000
Simon Property Group	2,441	16	4,020
Equity Residential	1,995	-14	6,400
Del Webb Corp.	1,936**	-5**	4,700*
Lincoln Property Co.	1,766	31	5,000
Wyndham Int'l	1,709	-18	26,000
Tishman Realty & Construction**	1,640	48	920
AIMCO	1,553	0	7,500
Vornado Realty Trust	1,541	34	1,422
The Irvine Co.**	1,500	15	470
Boston Properties	1,433	37	675
Brookfield Properties	1,372	-43	1,300
FelCor Lodging Trust	1,318	10	65

Continued next page

Key Real Estate Companies by 2002 Revenue (*cont'd.*)

Company	Revenue ($M)	% Change from 2001	# of Employees
CBRE Holding/CB Richard Ellis**	1,171	-12	9,700
The Rouse Co.	1,145	15	3,453
Crescent Real Estate Equities	1,109	48	671
MeriStar Hospitality Corp.	984	-9	30
Duke Realty Corp.	956	12	1,001
Trizec Properties	947	49	1,045
Cushman & Wakefield	870	6	11,000
Jones Lang LaSalle	840	-5	16,900
Archstone-Smith Trust	829	2	3,300

*2000 figures; ** 2001 figures. Sources: Hoovers.com; WetFeet analysis.

Additional Resources

Hoover's Real Estate Industry Snapshot

(http://www.hoovers.com/industry/snapshot/profile/0,3519,35,00.html)

Knowledge @ Wharton: Real Estate

(http://knowledge.wharton.upenn.edu/category.cfm?catid=8)

Institute of Real Estate Management (http://www.irem.org)

Realtor.org (http://www.realtor.org)

Semiconductors

Industry Overview

Semiconductors are the integrated-circuit (IC) chips that control everything from PCs and cellular phones to aircraft navigational systems and elevators. (Technically, semiconductors, primarily doped silicon, are the key raw ingredients of ICs, but the term has come to refer to the chips themselves, too.) Increasingly, ICs are showing up in every imaginable electronic consumer good, from toys to refrigerators. Partly because semiconductor manufacture is very capital intensive, the industry regularly faces temporary slumps and shakeouts. In spite of this, however, the industry should grow over the long term—as will the industry's thirst for engineers and other qualified personnel.

Integrated circuits contain millions of transistors and perform a wide range of functions: Logic chips do mathematical calculations, signal processors decode music and video, memory chips store information, microprocessors run computers and other devices, and controller chips run electronic devices such as VCRs or printers. Within the IC world, Intel is the dominant player; Advanced Micro Devices is another important player.

A smaller but faster-growing segment is digital signal processors, the stand-alone microprocessors used in cell phones and PC modems, which some estimate will be a $50 billion market in the next decade. Texas Instruments dominates this market, with Analog Devices and Motorola chasing it, among others. More and more intellectual property is going onto chips, increasing their functions and giving them even greater applications, especially in consumer electronics. This industry segment should grow to huge proportions as more digital products are developed.

Other semiconductor industry manufacturing segments include logic chips, microcontrollers, and flash memory.

This industry has its own law. Gordon Moore, one of Intel's founders, predicted the power of microprocessors would double every 18 months. Known throughout the industry as Moore's Law, this pronouncement has largely held true since he made it in 1965. By virtue of this doubling—and the applications that this increase in power has made possible—the semiconductor industry has thrived.

The semiconductor industry has a binary relationship to the technology industry, and so has seen its fair share of contraction along with the tech bust. For now, its immediate outlook is uncertain, but with the continued proliferation of technology in our everyday lives, semiconductor production should pick up when consumer spending does.

Trends

Telecommunications. Semiconductors used to be the brains of the computer industry. They are fast becoming the brains of many industries, affecting the telecommunications sphere most of all. Thanks to the low cost of the wireless chip, cellular phones are becoming almost as prevalent as the regular old land phone in the United States; in Europe they are even more so. And in underdeveloped nations where the high cost of implementing telephone wire infrastructure prohibits many households from acquiring phone service, cell phones are allowing communication to become more universal.

Spreading applications. More and more products are being made with microprocessors inside—from cars, which use chips to control a variety of functions including air bag deployment and anti-lock brakes, to small appliances. The world of science is benefiting from the low cost and high

performance of semiconductor-driven technology, for instance in conducting research on genes, where keeping track of the sheer number of possibilities requires computerized help. A whole range of medical diagnostic tools, such as MRI and ultrasound, depend on semiconductor-based equipment. And at the other end of the usefulness spectrum there are pens that contain digital clocks and greeting cards that make music courtesy of a microchip inside. No doubt, microchips will spread into more and more parts of our lives in the years to come.

Rebound? Not yet. The economic downturn has been very hard on the semiconductor industry. Corporate spending on chips plummeted with the decline, and semiconductor orders all but dried up. Indeed, in 2001 semiconductor revenue fell by nearly a third. While business improved a bit in 2002, many companies are back down to revenue levels that they last saw in 1997 or 1998. And fab, or chip factory, utilization rates continue to be weak. It may not be until 2004, or beyond, that the industry enjoys a true recovery.

Innovative products. While the picture's bleak in the short term, in the longer term things are brighter. One driver of this outlook: innovation. The semiconductor industry continues to develop. Sometime sooner or later, 64-bit chips will replace 32-chip chips as the standard for PCs. And new markets, such as the one for ferroelectric chips, which will provide enhanced performance for mobile phones and other products with wireless features, hold a lot of promise.

Unlikely partners. This is traditionally a very competitive industry. So it's a bit of a surprise that some traditional competitors have been collaborating on a variety of projects. Advanced Micro Devices, Infineon, and United Microtechnologies are now working together; so are Motorola, Philips, STMicroelectronics, and Taiwan Semiconductor. This is a sign of difficult economic times.

How It Breaks Down

Chipmakers. From the early days of the industry, talented engineers have had a passport to travel—ex-Fairchild Semiconductor execs (including Moore) left to form companies like Intel. Even today, top design engineers with great ideas can go into business for themselves, setting up small design shops and selling their designs. However, over the last several decades, the cost of going into—or staying in—the manufacturing end of the business has become huge. Today, a fab, or chip factory, costs more than $1 billion to build. As a result, chip fabrication forms its own segment of the industry and is populated by a relatively small number of huge players, including the microprocessor and memory chipmakers (like Intel, Motorola, IBM, Texas Instruments, and Micron) and ASIC (Application Specific IC) makers like IBM and LSI Logic.

Fabless. At the other end of the spectrum are the fabless shops, such as Xilinx and Broadcom, which tend to focus on design rather than manufacturing. These companies either outsource production of their chips to the companies with fabs or rely on sales of intellectual property (i.e., chip design) to the growing number of companies seeking to license specific designs. The fabless segment includes makers of PLD (programmable logic devices—chips that can be programmed after being created)—and the numerous small design shops that have been started by design engineers who have left the bigger players. Although these companies lack the stability of the bigger companies in the mature segments, there are more possibilities for growth here and often a good chance that a company might be acquired by one of the bigger companies.

Foundries. Some companies leave the design of chips to others, whether that means chipmakers outsourcing part of their manufacturing or fables players, and focus only on the manufacture of semiconductor products. The biggest players here are the Asian companies Taiwan Semiconductor and United Microelectronics.

Semiconductor manufacturing equipment. The semiconductor industry relies on the multibillion-dollar semiconductor manufacturing equipment (SME) sector for the equipment used to manufacture and test semiconductors. This sector follows the roughly four-year boom-and-bust cycle of the semiconductor market. Its leading player is Applied Materials, which makes wafer-fabrication equipment, among other products; Cadence Design Systems and Mentor Graphics, which focus on electronic design automation (a rapidly growing segment); and Photronics, which creates the quartz plates used as stencils to transfer circuit patterns onto wafers during production. A subset of the SME sector is testing equipment; KLA-Tencor and Teradyne are leaders in this area. Finally, an overview of the industry would be incomplete without mentioning the companies that manufacture packaging such as OSE USA and distributors such as Arrow Electronics.

Key Jobs for MBAs

Jobs fall into two general areas: technical and nontechnical. About 80 percent of the jobs in this industry are on the technical side. Salary levels listed below are base salaries only; compensation generally exceeds the base.

Project manager or product manager. This position manages a cross-functional team, acting as a mini-general manager of a product while managing pricing, promotion, and definition; determining customers; and facing competition. The project manager enhances and manages the product over time. This job requires five years of experience or an MBA and a technical background.

Salary range: $60,000 to $90,000.

Management, director level. This could involve managing product managers, planning future product launches, managing strategic-marketing initiatives, or directing field operations. Requires six to ten years of experience.

Salary range: $90,000 to $150,000.

Key Semiconductor Companies by 2002 Revenue

Company	Revenue ($M)	% Change from 2001	# of Employees
Samsung Electronics	33,987	25	n/a
Intel Corp.	26,764	1	78,700
Motorola	26,679	-11	97,000
Solectron	12,276	-34	73,000
Sanmina-SCI Corp.	8,762	116	46,030
Texas Instruments	8,383	2	34,589
STMicroelectronics	6,318	-1	43,170
Philips Semiconductors	5,457	-7	33,000*
Infineon Technologies	5,136	-9	30,423
Applied Materials	5,062	-31	16,077
Taiwan Semiconductor	4,645	28	13,676*
Jabil Circuit	3,546	-18	20,000
Tokyo Electron	3,150	-45	10,171
Hynix Semiconductors*	3,004	-57	13,036
IBM Microelectonics	2,800	n/a	21,500*
Advanced Micro Devices	2,697	-31	12,146
Micron Technologies	2,589	-34	18,700
United Microelectronics	1,939	-3	8,543*
LSI Logic	1,817	2	5,281
Analog Devices	1,708	-25	8,600
KLA-Tencor Corp.	1,637	-22	5,700
Cadence Design Systems	1,293	-10	5,175
Teradyne	1,222	-15	7,200
Xilinx	1,016	-39	2,611
Broadcom Corp.	1,083	13	2,589

*2001 figures. Sources: Hoovers.com; WetFeet analysis.

Additional Resources

Chip Directory (http://www.xs4all.nl/~ganswijk/chipdir)

Fabless Semiconductor Association (http://www.fsa.org)

Semiconductor Equipment & Materials International
(http://www.semi.org)

Telecommunications

Industry Overview

Telecommunications has made it possible to speak to or exchange text and images with virtually anyone in the world by pushing a few buttons. This immediacy of communication has had dramatic effects. It has made worldwide commerce easier; it has made totalitarian regimes more vulnerable to dissenting voices carried by fax or e-mail; it has made shopping more convenient. High-tech telecommunications in particular, including fax, e-mail, and wireless phones, let families and friends stay in contact more easily and less expensively. As reference material moves online, the Web makes academic and business research possible with less need to go to a physical library.

Telecommunications is a mammoth industry, encompassing companies that make hardware, produce software, and provide services. Hardware includes a vast range of products that enable communication across the entire planet,

from video broadcasting satellites to telephone handsets to fiber-optic transmission cables. Services include running the switches that control the phone system, making access to the Internet available, and configuring private networks by which international corporations conduct business. Software makes it all work, from sending and receiving e-mail to relaying satellite data to controlling telephone switching equipment.

The breakup of AT&T in 1984 created the modern telecommunications industry, subjecting phone companies to free-market forces for the first time. The long-distance market became competitive almost immediately, but the so-called Baby Bells have fought a rear-guard action against letting companies like AT&T or MCI Worldcom enter the local phone market. The Telecommunications Act of 1996 deregulated local phone markets. Proponents say deregulation will make telecommunications services more competitive, benefiting consumers. Critics say it will give a few, giant companies untrammeled sway over our ability to communicate with each other.

Telecom companies built staff and infrastructure like crazy during the boom times of the 1990s. These days, they're suffering from costs related to over capacity as the markets for their goods and services have not continued to grow at expected rates, due to the downturn in the economy. This has in turn hurt telecom-equipment providers, which suffered through a 15 percent decline in revenue in 2001. Most in the industry are struggling to ride out the storm, cutting costs via layoffs and other measures and trying to make it through to the point in the future when demand picks up. Some companies are not going to make it—and even industry behemoths are at risk (WorldCom, for example, declared bankruptcy in 2002). And even if the company you go to work for is not in immediate danger of going out of business, weak stock performance by many companies has made them more attractive as acquisition candidates—so don't expect your work place to look the same for very long.

Longer term, though, the outlook is good. The imminent rise in high-speed data services, voice communications over the Internet, and data networks will all mean more R&D, competition and, as leaders emerge, consolidation. As technology advances, the need for electrical and electronics engineers, computer software engineers, support and systems analysts will continue to grow.

Trends

Maturation of the cellular market. In just a decade, cellular telecommunications has become a mature market in the United States. The market is already huge—there are 130 million cell-phone owners in the United States—so there's no longer so much room for growth in the sector. Indeed, experts project an annual increase in cellular-program sign-ups of just 15 to 20 percent this year, compared to 50 percent annual increases in years past. The great hope for companies in the wireless sector is for growth in areas like wireless Internet services and text messaging (which is huge in Europe and Asia, but has not really caught on in the United States yet, probably due to a lack of technology standards that allow interaction between users of different wireless services).

A new meaning for "convergence." Even the big long-distance carriers want to get into the local phone-service ring—and because of deregulation, they're starting to do just that. The reason is that local service has higher margins than long distance. Meanwhile, the Baby Bells are trying to build their residential long-distance businesses; indeed, Verizon now offers long distance in six states, and SBC does the same in five states). The Baby Bells are also trying to hone in on the lucrative long-distance market, where AT&T makes $28 billion annually. Increased competition simultaneous with financial difficulties throughout the industry makes for a wild and woolly ride for those in telecom.

How It Breaks Down

Prior to the Telecommunications Act of 1996, a variety of regulations divided telecommunications artificially—cable TV companies were prohibited from offering local telephone service, video programming over phone lines was banned, and local service companies and long-distance service providers were forbidden from competing in each other's markets. The Telecommunications Act lifted these competitive restrictions. One regulatory barrier that remains prohibits service providers from manufacturing telecommunications equipment. The cleanest way to break this industry down, then, is between those who make the software and hardware and those who provide various services.

Service providers. These companies provide local and long-distance wireline telephone service. Industry insiders call this POTS, for plain old telephone service. Wireline providers include the large long-distance service providers—AT&T, MCI, and Sprint—and the RBOCs (the Baby Bells) like SBC Communications and BellSouth. A new generation of companies is laying fiber-optic wire networks to handle the rapidly increasing data traffic, including Qwest and Level 3.

Wireless service providers. Marked by carrier consolidation and partnering to augment geographic reach and gain economies of scale, wireless communication services have shaken up the telecom service industry. They have also brought telecommunications to the far corners of the earth, including parts of Africa and South America where there's no existing wireline infrastructure, and have made local markets far more competitive in the United States.

Satellite telecommunication services. Satellite telecom services breaks down into fixed satellite services such as INTELSAT; low earth orbit companies (LEOs), which include Iridium and mega-LEO Teledesic (controlled by Craig McCaw); direct broadcast satellite companies such as DIRECTV; and the global positioning system (GPS). Satellite services include everything from navigation systems (such as you can expect to find in the dash of your automobile sometime in the near future) to video broadcast and data transmission.

Internet service providers (ISPs). These consist of those companies that make it possible for you to go online—Microsoft, AOL, MindSpring, and the RBOCs. The Internet, which has become an integral part of the telecommunications industry, is also the vehicle by which a huge dose of talent and energy has been added to telecom as voice and data networks converge.

Customer premise equipment (CPE) manufacturers. Telecommunication service providers are the biggest customers of telecommunications equipment makers. When they sell a service to a company, for instance, they purchase the switch, which can serve anywhere from 15 to 100,000 people, as well as other customer premise equipment (CPE)—everything from telephones to voice-mail systems to private branch exchanges (PBXs). Local area networks (LAN) require their own routers, switches, and hubs. The big players here include Lucent Technologies, Nortel, Fujitsu, Siemens, and Alcatel.

Networking equipment and fiber optics manufacturers. Networking equipment includes the stuff that makes the local area network operative, including routers, hubs, switches, and servers. Fiber optics consists of the optical fiber and fiber-optic cable, transmitters, receivers, and connectors that carry data and voice messages. The biggest switch makers are Nortel and Lucent. Cisco and 3Com are among the biggest makers of networking equipment.

Wireless and satellite communication equipment manufacturers. These are different categories that we've grouped together. The radio-based communications systems, the switches, transmission, and subscriber equipment for this sector differ from those the wireline service providers use. Large players in wireless equipment include Motorola, Qualcomm, Hughes Electronics, Sony, and NEC. Satellite communication equipment makers include Comcast and Loral Space, as well as a number of cable companies, such as Cox Communications, DIRECTV, EchoStar Communications, and TCI International.

Key Jobs for MBAs

Product manager. Essentially, product managers make the product happen. Product managers determine what service or product they'll sell to the end user, then help develop it, be it wireless service, DSL, caller ID, or voice mail. On the manufacturing side, they need to know the technology or show some knowledge about it. This position generally requires an MBA or similar experience with another company, preferably in networking or data communications.

Salary range: $70,000 to $90,000.

Public relations and government relations. The role the government has played in regulating telecommunications has resulted in a number of jobs within the major companies to work with the government and press to enhance relations. These include lobbying government officials, helping draft legislation, and working with the press to garner favorable coverage for regulations your company supports.

Salary range: $50,000 to $150,000.

Key Telecommunications Companies by 2002 Revenue

Company	Revenue ($M)	% Change from 2001	# of Employees
Verizon Communications	67,625	1	229,500
SBC Communications	43,138	-6	175,400
NEC Corp.	38,446	-11	142,000
AT&T	37,827	-28	71,000
Fujitsu Limited	37,748	-13	170,111
Nokia	31,526	13	53,849*
Motorola	26,679	-11	97,000
Sprint	26,634	2	72,200
BT Group	26,293	-9	108,600
Siemens	25,989	14	162,000
BellSouth	22,440	-7	77,000
Cellco Partnership	19,260	11	39,300
Cisco Systems	18,915	-15	36,000
Alcatel	17,379	-23	99,000*
Ericcson	16,808	-24	85,000*
AT&T Wireless Services	15,631	15	31,000
Qwest Communications	15,487	-21	61,000*
Cingular Wireless	14,727	4	33,800
Comcast Holdings	12,460	29	82,000
Lucent Technologies	12,321	-43	47,000
Sprint PCS Group	12,074	24	28,000
Nortel Networks	10,560	-40	36,960
Nextel Communications	8,721	13	14,900
ALLTEL Corp.	7,983	5	25,348
DIRECTV	7,193	14	n/a

*2001 figures. Sources: Fortune.com; Hoovers.com; WetFeet analysis.

Industries

Additional Resources

CrossNodes (http://networking.earthweb.com)

Hoover's Wireless Services Industry Snapshot
(http://www.hoovers.com/industry/snapshot/profile/0,3519,49,00.html)

Hoover's Telecommunications Services Industry Snapshot
(http://www.hoovers.com/industry/snapshot/profile/0,3519,41,00.html)

Hoover's Telecommunications Equipment Industry Snapshot
(http://www.hoovers.com/industry/snapshot/profile/0,3519,57,00.html)

McKinsey Quarterly: Telecom
(http://www.mckinseyquarterly.com/category_editor.asp?L2=22)

Telecommunications Online (http://www.telecoms-mag.com)

Venture Capital

Industry Overview

VC firms raise money from corporations, financial institutions, private foundations, university endowments, and wealthy individuals. The money—sometimes as much as several hundred million dollars—goes into funds, which are invested in start-ups in return for a share of ownership. When the start-up

goes public or gets acquired, the investment is cashed in for huge profits. Typically, the VC firm distributes 75 to 80 percent of the return to the original investors and keeps 20 to 25 percent for itself. Sometimes the start-up goes nowhere and the investors lose money.

VC funding has nourished some of corporate America's greatest success stories when they were still baby businesses—FedEx, Intel, Sun Microsystems, and Apple, to name a few. Once a VC firm has sorted through stacks of business plans and selected a few lucky companies to invest in, the firm's partners usually help those firms by arranging services, introducing contacts, setting up strategic partnerships, and often taking seats on their boards of directors. The VC firm usually hopes for an exit event—an IPO or acquisition that will let the VC firm cash out—in about five years from the time it invests.

In the midst of a slowing economy, the VC industry is undergoing tremendous change. In the late 1990s, venture capitalists focused primarily on high-tech companies to meet their lofty return-on-capital goals, investing an astronomical $104.2 billion in start-ups alone, according to the National Venture Capital Association. But with online retailers closing up shop and Internet IPOs more rare than steak tartare, many VC funds are turning their full attention to areas such as biotech. With tight funding and a slew of failing Internet companies in their portfolios, venture capital firms are exercising much more caution, investing warily and with less money.

The venture capital industry is small and hires only a select few each year. Traditionally dominated by seasoned executives, many firms consist only of general partners and administrative staff, though some larger firms also have associates and analysts. However, even large firms may have only one associate for every three partners. In the active market of recent years, VC firms increased hiring at junior levels; but there is far less new investment activity now, resulting in fewer employment opportunities.

Trends

Down-rounding the dot coms. As the NASDAQ suffers, VC firms have a lot of cleaning up to do. Most poured millions into Internet start-ups in 1999 and 2000, and as these companies flounder or fold, venture capitalists face some tough choices. Many of the 200 or so Internet-driven VC firms launched in the past few years have gone bankrupt. And more-resilient VC funds are shutting down their failing start-ups by pulling out of the next round of funding needed to keep them afloat, or holding back funds until the venture shows survival signs. A couple of years ago, start-ups could pick and choose their favorite VCs; now firms are consolidating their portfolios and doling out "down rounds," much lower valuations of funding, to surviving ventures fighting for investor support.

Industry shakeout in progress. Venture investments dropped 65 percent between 2000 and 2001 as the stock market downturn slammed the lucrative IPO window shut and slashed the valuations of both public and private companies. In Q4 2000, VCs saw the first negative quarterly return for the industry (-6.3 percent) since 1998.

Things have not gotten better. The 300 mergers and acquisitions of VC-backed companies in 2002 were 12 percent fewer than in 2001, worth $7.2 billion compared to $17.1 billion. VC fundraising dropped from $38 billion in 2001 to $8 billion in 2002. Investments in the industry's biggest sectors, including software, networking, biotech, and telecommunications, all declined. Star VC John Doerr from Kleiner Perkins even apologized for once calling the Internet "the largest legal creation of wealth in the history of the planet."

According to Venture Economics (VE) and the NVCA, a rebound is still several years away. "There is too much money in VC," says an insider. "What we're doing now is waiting for the time our industry recovers, and that will be measured in years, not quarters."

How It Breaks Down

There are many kinds of players in the VC world, from traditional VC firms to funds operated by publicly owned corporations. Some are tightly focused—by stage of investment, region, or type of industry—but most have a much broader focus. Here's a rough breakdown of the industry:

Private VC firms (early- to mid-stage). Firms in this segment follow the classic VC model: Find an entrepreneur with a great idea and business plan, sprinkle with cash, bake for several years, and sell for a hefty chunk of change. Early-stage (or seed) investments are the riskiest, since many start-ups tank. Still, they often provide the highest returns since investors coming in early can pay a lower price for a given share of equity. In the 1990s, as many traditional VC firms started to focus on middle- and late-stage investments, seed financing increasingly became the province of newer firms and angel investors—entrepreneurs or corporate executives who've made it big and have money to spend.

Private VC firms (mid- to late stage). These firms, many of which also operate at the seed level, provide funds to companies that are already established—those that have a product, sufficient employees, and perhaps even revenues. At these stages, firms inject more capital into the company to help it become profitable so that it will attract enough interest to either be acquired by a larger company or go public.

Growth buyout funds. Some VCs have moved into growth buyouts of larger private companies or divisions of public companies. These funds invest larger amounts of capital—up to $100 million—in exchange for a significant minority or majority position in the company. By focusing on stable, growing (and often profitable) companies, buyout funds don't have to wait long before they can cash in on the company's IPO or sale. There's less risk—unless market factors

cause the delay of an IPO, for example. The funded company and its earlier investors benefit from having a prestigious late-stage investor add credibility on Wall Street come IPO time.

Financial-services firms. Where there's money, of course you'll find I-bankers. Banks such as Morgan Stanley and Citicorp will invest in the later stages. The aim is pretty much the same as that of the VCs: to make a killing through either an IPO or an acquisition.

Corporate funds. As opposed to private funds, whose primary goal is monetary gain, corporate funds have the added goal of strategically investing in companies whose business relates in some way to the corporation's own. For example, Microsoft invested in Qwest Communications, a telecom company that is building a fiber-optic network, to help it deliver NT-based software.

Key Jobs for MBAs

Staffing needs and titles vary greatly from one venture capital firm to the next. Many funds consist solely of partners and support staff. Others hire a limited number of undergraduates and MBAs as analysts and associates with the expectation that most will return to get their business degrees or join start-ups within a few years. (Keep in mind that while the terms "analyst" and "associate" usually refer to undergrads and MBAs or experienced hires, respectively, at some firms the titles are reversed.) Even at the lowest professional levels, compensation is tied to the performance of the fund. But because of built-in fund-management fees, no one ever starves at a venture capital firm—and as a rule, venture capitalists do very well for themselves. Top-tier partners at major funds are worth many millions of dollars. Lower-level professional staff and junior partners can expect total compensation exceeding (often vastly exceeding) $250,000 per year. Compensation at corporate venture funds is lower.

General partner. These are the people with their names on the door. General partners raise the money for the fund and make the final decisions on which companies to invest in. General partners, the professional members of a venture capital firm, are usually required to contribute a small amount of their own money to their fund. They manage the fund's investments and generally take a 20 to 30 percent cut of the carry from the fund. General partners are expected to provide a wealth of business advice and industry contacts to the entrepreneurs they back. They often sit on the boards of many companies and are deeply involved in decisions about "exit strategies"—that is, when to cash out by taking the company public or selling it.

Salary range: $200,000 to $500,000 and up, plus the potential of millions in profits.

Junior partner. Junior partners are just that: junior versions of the general partners. Usually, junior partnerships are viewed as training for general partnerships and junior partners perform similar duties albeit on a reduced scale. Also reduced is their personal stake in the fund itself.

Salary range: $150,000 to $300,000, plus a limited amount of carry, or percentage of profits.

VP or associate. Some firms hire MBAs or people with business experience (usually in leveraged buyouts or investment banking) as vice presidents or associates. Associates screen business plans, make cold calls on prospective investments, and on occasion make on-site visits to portfolio companies. At this level, compensation, while still tied to the overall performance of the fund, can take the form of a flat bonus rather than a percentage of the fund.

Salary range: $75,000 to $250,000, including bonus; VPs earn at the higher end.

Key Venture Capital Firms by Number of Deals in Q1 2003

Company	# of Deals Closed	Headquarters
New Enterprise Associates	17	Baltimore, MD
Austin Ventures	13	Austin, TX
Intel Capital	13	Santa Clara, CA
Venrock Associates	13	New York, NY
Warburg Pincus	13	New York, NY
Morgenthaler Ventures	11	Menlo Park, CA
TL Ventures	11	Wayne, PA
Draper Fisher Jurvetson	10	Redwood City, CA
J.P. Morgan Partners	10	New York, NY
Sevin Rosen Funds	10	Dallas, TX
Advanced Technology Ventures	9	Waltham, MA
Mayfield Fund	9	Menlo Park, CA
North Bridge Venture Partners	9	Waltham, MA
Prism Venture Partners	9	Westwood, MA
Sigma Partners	9	Menlo Park, CA
Accel Partners	8	Palo Alto, CA
Crescendo Venture Mgmt	8	Palo Alto, CA
Atlas Venture	7	Waltham, MA
Bessemer Venture Partners	7	Wellesley Hills, MA
Canaan Partners	7	Rowayton, CT
Enterprise Partners	7	La Jolla, CA
Flagship Ventures	7	Cambridge, MA
Granite Ventures	7	San Francisco, CA
Mobius Venture Capital	7	Palo Alto, CA
Oxford Bioscience Partners	7	Boston, MA

Continued next page

Key Venture Capital Firms by Number of Deals in Q1-03 (*cont'd.*)

Company	# of Deals Closed	Headquarters
Stonehenge Capital Corp.	7	Baton Rouge, LA
VantagePoint Venture Partners	7	San Bruno, CA
Zero Stage Capital	7	Cambridge, MA
Columbia Capital	6	Alexandria, VA
Domain Associates	6	Princeton, NJ
Polaris Venture Partners	6	Waltham, MA
Redpoint Ventures	6	Menlo Park, CA
Sequoia Capital	6	Menlo Park, CA
St. Paul Venture Capital	6	Eden Prairie, MN

Source: PricewaterhouseCoopers Money Tree Survey.

Additional Resources

Harvard Business School Venture Capital & Principal Investment Club
(http://sa.hbs.edu/vc)

National Venture Capital Association (http://www.nvca.org)

PricewaterhouseCoopers Money Tree Survey
(http://www.pwcmoneytree.com)

VentureReporter.net (http://venturereporter.net)

Careers

WetFeet®

Asset Management

Career Overview

Asset managers manage money—other people's money, and gobs of it. Generally, they convert that money into assets—stocks, bonds, derivatives, and other types of investments—and try to make that money make more money as fast as possible. Mutual funds, for instance, hire asset managers; so do corporations with lots of money sitting around, banks, and high net-worth individuals.

Asset managers have one simple goal: to invest other people's money wisely and profitably. Asset managers use a combination of investment theory, quantitative tools, market experience, research, and plain dumb luck to pick investments for their portfolios, ranging from high-risk stocks to commercial real estate to cash accounts.

As soon as they've picked their basket of investments, they've stuck their necks out on the block. And the ax will fall if the portfolio doesn't beat its benchmark—a peer group (competitor funds with the same investment objective), or a market index (e.g., the S&P 500).

Requirements

As an asset manager, you can't just bet your hunches. The profession requires excellent quantitative and analytical skills—if you hated statistics, you may want to look elsewhere.

But asset management isn't just a matter of adding up the numbers. It requires the organizational skills—and nerve—to make split-second decisions with millions of dollars riding on the line. And though the profession has seen tremendous growth in the last decade, it's still tough to break into, especially for those who only have an undergraduate degree. Sometimes MBAs work as fund managers right out of school, though more often they start as analysts in order to prove they have the right combination of caution and chutzpah to make a great asset manager.

Competition for jobs is fierce at all levels, but if you have strong quantitative and analytical skills, good nerves, and can consistently beat the market, then there's probably a place for you. Networking and a single-minded pursuit of your goal are big helps, too.

Generally, MBAs come aboard as researchers or analysts. Sometimes they're hired as fund managers, but only if they have a track record of success as both managers and investors. Because competition is tough, it's important to know a lot about the company interviewing you, and to show an intimate knowledge of its investment strategies.

Analysts and researchers generally serve at least two years before they come up for consideration as fund managers. You are also more likely to get an asset-manager position earlier if you run smaller portfolios for institutional asset managers or private banks that offer services to the wealthy. On the mutual-fund side, you might become co-portfolio manager, sharing the management responsibility with a senior manager. The larger the pool of assets, the fiercer the competition.

There is no single prerequisite to becoming an asset manager. It all comes down to how much money you can make with other people's money. That said, virtually all successful asset managers possess these skills:

Copyright 2003 WetFeet, Inc.

151

Quantitative and analytical skills. Asset managers have to be able to read spreadsheets and earnings reports. And they have to be able to take those numbers and crunch them into financial models and future projections. Even if you're dealing with less volatile investments such as bonds or real estate, you have to do the math in order to stay ahead of conventional wisdom. Classes in accounting and statistics are a big help, as are jobs that require number crunching, from I-banking to management consulting.

Managerial and organizational skills. Whether you're a researcher or a fund manager, you'll have to keep track of reams of facts in order to glean the really important information. Furthermore, you'll have to be able to make decisions—and execute them—quickly and accurately. Delay can cost big money. Finally, you need to be able to motivate and manage a talented staff of researchers and analysts if you work your way up to portfolio manager. Without their coordinated efforts, you may not have the information you need to make the best decision possible.

Professional licensing. In general, asset managers who work behind the scenes and make the big decisions don't need professional licensing. But if you're dealing with the public at all, you probably will, especially if you're in a position to make buy and sell recommendations directly to a client. For example, you may need an NASD license (Series 7, 63, or 65), or certain insurance licenses. Employers will generally give you the time to get such licenses once you're hired, and may even pay the costs.

Career tracks

Mutual funds, such as Vanguard or T. Rowe Price, are perhaps the most visible road into asset management. Hedge funds—which specialize in high-risk, high-return investments for wealthy clients—also offer opportunities for would-be asset managers.

Large investment and commercial banks, from J.P. Morgan Chase to Citibank, as well as private firms such as Soros Fund Management, offer private banking—that is, asset management for wealthy clients with very large private accounts. Some large-scale investment institutions such as universities and retirement funds hire their own investment staffs, though often they rely on mutual funds and other investment management companies to make decisions for them, from Fidelity to the Capital Group.

If you prefer real estate to stocks and bonds, you can work for a real estate investment trust (REIT) such as Cornerstone Properties. REITs operate like mutual funds, except they buy and sell hotels and shopping malls rather than stocks and bonds. Finally, there are a number of boutique asset-management firms that take money from a small group of wealthy clients and invest in specialized areas such as start-up companies.

No matter where you work, asset management boils down to this: researching and analyzing potential investments and deciding where exactly to allocate funds. Of course, companies require a raft of other employees, including corporate managers, IT specialists, marketing and sales people, and back-office staff. But if you want to be on the front lines where big investment decisions are made, you will fulfill one of these three functions:

Researcher. The job of the researcher is implied in the name: He or she gathers the primary source material from which investment decisions are made, such as SEC filings and quarterly earning reports. When they start, researchers spend their time learning what those running the portfolio emphasize. Asset management companies that hire fund managers pursue different investment philosophies, and researchers work to ensure that the fund manager has the information necessary to make the decisions he or she needs to make with that philosophy in mind.

As time passes, researchers are granted more independence, and may even perform the kind of higher-level analyses that lead to actual decisions about buying and selling. Generally, researchers are hired straight out of undergraduate or B-school programs. MBAs, of course, enjoy better odds of getting hired and generally command better salaries. All candidates should have strong quantitative, analytical, and organizational skills.

Analyst. There is a gray area between the work of a researcher and that of an analyst. However, analysts are definitely higher up in the decision-making chain, and typically manage researchers (if a firm has researchers). Analysts take the work of researchers and apply higher-level financial modeling in order to make specific recommendations to portfolio managers about which securities to buy or sell.

In addition to crunching numbers, they may conduct more subjective research, such as meeting with representatives of potential investment companies in order to assess management style. Or they may pick the brains of sell-side analysts at brokerages and other financial institutions to gather tips about specific investments and to gauge overall market trends. Seasoned analysts may even participate in developing overall investment strategies for their investment fund.

Fund manager. Basically, fund managers are the people who decide what, when, and how much to buy or sell. They must work to ensure that their fund's overall investment philosophy is borne out in actual investments, and be willing to change course midstream if their strategy isn't working. They must also make sure their decisions are executed, which means following up on the work of traders and other agents. And of course they're responsible for managing the work of researchers and analysts in order to ensure that the fund manager is receiving the best, most complete information possible.

Besides poring over numbers, they spend a great deal of time meeting with managers of companies they might invest in to make more subjective, managerial assessments. Finally, they may have to engage in a certain amount of marketing and public relations—for example, helping to design sales strategies or talking to the press.

Additional Resources

Financial Analysts Journal (http://www.aimrpubs.org/faj/home.html)

Knowledge @ Wharton: Finance and Investment
(http://knowledge.wharton.upenn.edu/category.cfm?catid=1)

Investors' Business Daily (http://www.investors.com)

Institutional Investor Online (http://www.institutionalinvestor.com)

McKinsey Quarterly: Financial Services
(http://www.mckinseyquarterly.com/category_editor.asp?L2=10)

Ohio State University List of Finance Sites
(http://www.cob.ohio-state.edu/fin/journal/jofsites.htm)

Business Development

Career Overview

Business development (also known as biz dev) is exactly what it sounds like: It involves figuring out how to build or develop a business. You can find business development jobs in all industries—at everything from tech start-ups to huge pharmaceuticals companies. What the work entails depends on how established a company is and what its business model is.

Business development people constantly ask: "What ten things will have the biggest positive impact on my company's business, and how can we make them happen?" Their objective is to expand the market reach or revenue of their companies in ways that make the most of their companies' resources and capabilities.

Biz dev executes the company's strategy by "doing deals" with complementary businesses. Exactly what that means varies from company to company. A deal might be a co-branding initiative, a technology- or content-licensing arrangement, an e-commerce partnership, or some combination of the three.

Business development involves varying degrees of sales and strategy. In some companies, biz dev people may focus on getting new corporate sales accounts, while in others they may lead new product development. At larger companies such as AOL Time Warner, Cisco, or Microsoft, one of biz dev's many responsibilities may be to decide which smaller companies the company should acquire next to ensure that it retains its market strength in the future.

Careers

Working in business development is an excellent way to become adept at business strategy while gaining hands-on experience in negotiating deals and managing partner relationships. Business development jobs are also highly cross-functional, requiring close collaboration with various internal and partner-company teams such as sales, engineering, and marketing to ensure that a deal is consummated. With its focus on strategy, biz dev steers the direction of a company-the deals forged today determine what the rest of the company will be working on tomorrow.

Requirements

If you're interested in business but don't want to go the traditional route of working for a consulting or investment-banking firm, biz dev may be a good alternative. The best way to get into business development is by first gaining experience in finance, consulting, or corporate sales. The minimum degree requirement for an entry-level position in business development is a BA or BS. For more senior positions, an MBA is often preferred, along with five or more years of previous business development or sales experience.

Business development positions at high-tech companies may require a technical background, or sales experience in a related field. Strategic-planning or corporate-development positions usually require a minimum of two years' experience in investment banking or consulting.

Networking with friends or alumni will give you an advantage getting your foot in the door. If you're asked in for an interview, be ready to demonstrate your knowledge of the company's business and show that you're familiar with its competitive landscape. Be sure to play up any experience you have in closing deals or managing relationships. And remember that recruiters will be seeking a keen eye for detail, solid communication skills, and analytical ability.

Career Tracks

In order of increasing sophistication, the three overlapping layers within business development are sales, partnerships, and strategic planning. Most biz dev jobs blend all three, although one area may be emphasized.

Sales. At some companies, business development might be better described as business-to-business sales. In many cases, the business development team and the sales team are one and the same.

Cold calling or prospecting for potential clients, members, or partners is often a task that falls to entry-level biz dev employees. These employees often have to hone their own "sales pitch" to convince other companies that a partnership would add value to their businesses.

As in traditional sales jobs, there's often an account-management aspect to business development—coordinating a variety of partner relationships and deal types, each at a different stage.

Partnerships. Companies of all sizes in all industries are building their businesses around partnerships—and it is business development's responsibility to initiate and manage such relationships.

Often the biggest challenge facing business developers is negotiating the terms of partnership deals. Getting another company interested in a partnership is just the beginning—drafting a contract and negotiating its terms is a process that can drag on for months.

Once both parties sign the contract, business development must work with other teams in a company (e.g., product management, marketing, and operations) to oversee the successful meeting of the terms of the partnership.

Careers

Strategic planning. Some business development jobs aren't called that at all. Instead, they're called "strategic planning," or sometimes "corporate development." Strategic-planning jobs are found mostly at large, established companies seeking to expand and diversify their business. Just like management consultants, strategic planners spend a lot of time thinking about top-level strategy issues such as what new business activities their company should pursue, how it should position itself and market those activities, and which technologies it should invest in.

At some companies, strategic planning may be carried out by the corporate finance department. In such cases, biz dev jobs may resemble investment-banking functions such as mergers and acquisitions. For instance, if a company wants to acquire a new business unit, strategic planning may analyze the market to find a suitable business to acquire, determine an appropriate asking price for the company, and follow through the negotiation process.

If the acquisition takes place, strategic planning may help integrate the two companies. This task may be as simple as processing a stack of paperwork or as complex as relocating and reorganizing the activities and personnel of the two companies.

Strategic planning may also involve institutional investment—that is, parceling out the company's money to fund outside start-ups. In this way, strategic planning can be a bit like working in the venture capital industry. For instance, when high-tech companies invest in high-tech start-ups, strategic planners may perform due diligence on potential partners, determine how much to invest in a particular venture, and negotiate a stake in a company.

Additional Resources

JustSell.com (http://www.justsell.com/)

McKinsey Quarterly: Alliances
(http://www.mckinseyquarterly.com/category_editor.asp?L2=25)

McKinsey Quarterly: Strategy
(http://www.mckinseyquarterly.com/category_editor.asp?L2=21)

National Association of Sales Professionals (http://www.nasp.com)

Technology Business Development Forum (http://www.ibdf.org)

Consulting

Career Overview

In the world of business, management consultants are jacks-of-all-trades. Working through consulting firms or as independent contractors, they advise corporations and other organizations regarding an infinite array of issues related to business strategy—from reengineering to e-commerce, change management to systems integration. From billion-dollar mergers and acquisitions to corporate reorganizations in which thousands of jobs are at stake, they are the directors behind the scenes of nearly every major event in the marketplace.

A career in consulting can encompass a wide variety of industries. Pretty much anybody with a specialty in a field can offer consulting service; to keep this profile specific, we've focused on management consulting, a broad category in its own right.

Most management consultants hold salaried positions at firms that cater to a clientele of mostly large corporations. They are assigned on a project basis to their firm's clients, who are billed by the hour for their services. Depending on the client's needs and the firm's functional specialty (or core competency, as it's often called), consultants conduct objective research and analysis on behalf of their client, and make recommendations based on their findings. Ultimately, management consultants take on the responsibility of improving their clients' businesses by affecting change through their recommendations.

Research and analysis are the main tools of the trade for management consultants. They analyze a business problem from various angles by conducting research, and forming and testing hypotheses. Research may consist of collecting raw data from internal sources—such as the client's computers or through interviewing the client's employees—and external sources, such as trade associations or government agencies. A consultant gets some of his or her most valuable data through surveys and market studies that they devise and implement themselves. The data must then be analyzed in relation to the client's organization, operations, customers, and competitors to locate potential areas for improvement and form solutions. These solutions are then recommended to the client and—hopefully—implemented. (Sometimes convincing a client to accept a consultant's recommendations can be the most difficult aspect of the job, and there is always a chance that the client may choose not to accept the consultant's recommendation at all.)

For those who enjoy problem solving and thinking about business strategy, consulting can be a very fulfilling career as well as an excellent jumping-off

Careers

point for a management career or a future as an entrepreneur. On the flip side, frequent travel and long hours can make a consultant's schedule very demanding.

While consulting is great for people who like variety in their work, it is not for those allergic to structure and hierarchy. The large and elite firms tend to have a culture that mirrors that of their corporate clients, complete with a steep career-ladder: Only a select few make it to partner-level, and that's with an MBA and six to eight years at the firm.

Requirements

Although the competition at top firms is intense, the qualities that recruiters look for are similar across the board. Besides outstanding academic records, firms want people who are problem solvers, creative thinkers, good communicators, and who have a keen understanding of and interest in business.

Top candidates will also have previous experience in the business world (consulting internships are impressive but not required) as well as a record of extracurricular achievement. Firms specializing in IT consulting or e-business may require technical skills and experience.

The recruiting process at the elite strategy firms and the Big Five-affiliated consulting firms is standard for undergraduates and MBAs at top schools, and begins on campuses in the fall. For those who are not in school (or not at one of the handful of schools where firms recruit), the recruiting process begins at the firms' websites, many of which offer online applications. Alternatively, interested candidates can mail their resumes and cover letters to firms directly or to the attention of the recruiting director at his or her preferred office location.

Candidates with experience in industry are much sought after, particularly by firms that have industry practices that correspond to candidates' backgrounds. Several firms hold specialized information sessions for experienced candidates as well as PhDs and JDs. Consult firms' websites directly or contact firms' human resources departments or local graduate schools for schedules and eligibility.

Recruiting at most consulting firms, particularly those with a heavy strategy orientation, is bound to include at least one case interview in which the candidate is asked to solve a made-up business problem. The interview is designed to test the candidate's problem-solving skills, understanding of basic business principles, and communication skills. While there's no one correct answer to most case questions, there are several tried-and-true approaches to solving them that recruiters look for. To learn more about case questions and how to crack them, get WetFeet's bestselling *Ace Your Case* Insider Guide series.

Most firms offer internships to highly qualified undergraduates and those enrolled in MBA programs. Competition for internships can be even more intense than for permanent positions, but a successful internship can dramatically increase a candidate's chances of getting an offer after graduation. Recruiting for internships generally begins on college campuses in the fall. For more information, consult firms' websites.

Career Tracks

People who want a career in consulting can find a number of attractive alternatives. To help you get a better handle on the options, we've grouped the consulting world into several different segments. Keep in mind, however, that such groupings are somewhat arbitrary. Firms in one group can and do compete directly with players in the other segments. Also, consolidation and growth are rapidly changing the landscape.

Elite management consulting firms. This group is populated by the elite strategy firms: McKinsey, Bain, Booz Allen Hamilton, and Boston Consulting Group, and a host of smaller challengers.

The bulk of these firms' work consists of providing chief executive officers in Fortune 500 companies with strategic or operational advice. For this, they charge the highest fees and earn the most prestige. They also have the fattest attitudes, work the most intense hours, and take home the most pay. These firms fight to woo the top recruits coming from the best graduate and undergraduate schools. Although some elite firms differentiate themselves by specializing in particular industries or functions, most consultants who work for this group of firms are generalists who work on a wide variety of projects and industries.

Big Five–affiliated consulting firms. Accenture, Deloitte Consulting, Cap Gemini Ernst & Young, BearingPoint (formerly KPMG Consulting), and IBM Business Consulting Services (which acquired PricewaterHouseCoopers Consulting)—these are the five consulting practices affiliated with, or descending from, the Big Five (now the Big Four with the demise of Arthur Andersen) of the accounting world. These firms provide a range of strategic advice, information-systems support, and other, more specialized consulting services to many of the same corporations served by the elite consulting firms. Most boast strong information-technology capabilities on projects requiring heavy systems-implementation work. They tend to be larger and more complex than the elite strategy firms. They also tend to keep their competitive eyes trained on each other rather than on the smaller firms in the field.

Though somewhat less prestigious than many of the elite firms, according to insiders, they are slightly less intense and significantly less hung up on themselves. The culture, workload, and atmosphere can vary greatly within a particular firm, from one practice group or office to the next.

Boutique strategy firms. Within the universe of strategy-and-operations consulting firms is a significant cohort of firms that specialize in a particular industry, process, or type of consulting. If you are interested in a particular industry or type of consulting, these firms offer excellent career opportunities.

Typically, they are smaller than the big-name strategy firms and work with a smaller, more specialized group of clients—so they won't usually require you to work in industries that don't interest you. Because of the acute specialization of these firms, consultants at boutiques cultivate a deeper and more focused understanding of a particular industry or business function than those at larger firms.

Representative players include: Advisory Board Company and APM (health care); Corporate Executive Board (cross-company research); DiamondCluster International (telecommunications and the internet); Marakon Associates (strategy); MarketBridge, formerly Oxford Associates (sales); PRTM (high-tech operations); Strategic Decisions Group (decision analysis); Roland Berger Strategy Consultants (strategy and operations).

Technology and systems consulting firms. If you have a strong inclination toward technology and love designing computer systems and applications, this may be the area for you. Firms in this sector, such as SAP, IBM, and PeopleSoft typically take on large projects to design, implement, and manage their clients' information and computer systems.

In contrast to pie-in-the-sky strategy consulting, which involves work that can often be done at a home office, technology consulting takes place in the bowels of the client organization, or, in many cases, completely off-site. A typical project might involve creating a new inventory tracking system for a national retailer. Such a project might include analyzing what information technology a client needs, acquiring new hardware, and writing computer code to run the new system.

Internet consulting firms. Internet consulting firms focus exclusively on helping companies do business and differentiate themselves on the Internet. Such firms offer a wide range of services, from concept to execution, including building e-commerce portals, writing Web marketing plans, creating content and software to facilitate online transactions, and analyzing clients' network infrastructure and management.

Recent years have brought tough times for Internet consultancies. Once-thriving firms such as Organic and Razorfish have lost a majority of their clientele to the dot-com decline and are barely in business. More and more Internet consultancies are cutting their losses and selling out to tech giants like IBM, which snatched up struggling e-consultancies Mainspring (and then subsequently acquired PwC's consulting unit). Most independent consulting firms have either vanished or been acquired by a larger company. For now at least, Internet consulting has stepped to the sidelines of information technology consulting overall.

Additional Resources

Consulting Central (http://www.consultingcentral.com)

Dowjones.com (http://www.dowjones.com)

Corporate Finance

Career Overview

If you work in private enterprise, your company measures its success at the end of the year by comparing how much money it made to how much it spent. If it has made more than it has spent, it was a good year. If it has made less than it has spent, it was a bad year—or the company is in an investment phase. (In other words, like Amazon.com, it spent more than it made because the company and its investors believed it would realize a profit in the near future.)

People who work in corporate finance and accounting are responsible for managing the money—forecasting where it will come from, knowing where it is, and helping managers decide how to spend it in ways that will ensure the greatest return.

This career profile focuses on opportunities in corporate finance and accounting in private industry.

Accounting concerns itself with day-to-day operations. Accountants balance the books, track expenses and revenue, execute payroll, and pay the bills. They also compile all the financial data needed to issue a company's financial statements in accordance with government regulations.

Finance pros analyze revenue and expenses to ensure effective use of capital. They also advise businesses about project costs, make capital investments, and structure deals to help companies grow.

In spite of their different roles, finance and accounting are joined at the hip: The higher levels of accounting (budgeting and analysis) blend in with financial functions (analysis and projections). Thus, finance and accounting are often treated as one, with different divisions undertaking particular tasks such as cash management or taxes.

Requirements

Finance and accounting jobs require critical, detail-oriented thinking. If you have a knack for using numbers to understand patterns that influence business, you're going to be valuable to a company. If you can't crunch and analyze them, this isn't going to be the right job for you. You should also like, and be good at, solving problems and be able to think critically about the numbers you're working with.

Finally, if you can effectively evaluate business scenarios and recommend a course of action based on quantitative research, finance may be just the career for you. Internships are always a great way to strengthen your resume and differentiate yourself from other candidates. An MBA will make you attractive to companies hiring for budgeting, planning, and strategy functions.

Many firms hire outstanding undergraduates and MBAs for training programs: some are finance and accounting specific, and others rotate trainees throughout the company. If you have your heart set on corporate finance and analysis, do a knockout job during that particular rotation and develop a good relationship with your manager.

If there is no formal program, you'll have to make the most of on-the-job training, so try to find a position that will expose you to a variety of projects. Find out what the career path in corporate finance is at your company and cultivate a mentor. A mentor can explain what projects will round out your

Careers

background and what courses you can take to prepare yourself for a higher level assignment. You can also check out job listings on the Web to see what kind of experience and certification the jobs you're interested in require.

If you want to pursue a lifelong career as a number-cruncher, you'll probably have to knuckle down and get an advanced degree or certification—a CPA, MBA, or CFA could all come into play—at least to work in the more senior budgeting, planning, and strategy functions. You'll also need to keep track of the regulatory changes that affect how information is reported.

There are other ways in: Experience with an investment-banking firm can lead to a financial-analysis position for a specific business line or to a corporate-development position if you have several years of experience. At the higher accounting tiers, one of the most straightforward routes to becoming a controller (a supervisory accounting role) is to start working for one of the large accounting or auditing firms and then go into corporate finance.

Career Tracks

Although conditions vary at different companies, people going into corporate finance generally start their careers either as staff accountants (for the corporate-reporting function) or as financial analysts (for a business group or function). In both roles, you'll supply management with the information it needs to make smart, opportune decisions.

Staff accountants consolidate information for the official corporate financial reports—primarily comparing the present to the past. Financial analysts, on the other hand, are assigned to either a product line or business unit. They help management set up profit objectives, analyze current unit results, and anticipate future financial performance. Over time, financial analysts and staff accountants eventually specialize in one of the areas described below.

General accounting. General accountants are responsible for producing all of the financial records a corporation uses to track its progress internally and to meet government regulations. Such workers also gather all the information needed to compute a company's balance sheet, profit and loss statements, and income statements. They also track the corporate budget, cash flow, and pay all the bills.

Usually, your first job in general accounting will be in accounts payable or accounts receivable. Success in accounting might lead you to a position as a controller, overseeing a larger group, aggregating information, or working on portions of the corporate budget.

Internal audit. When most people think of an audit, they think of an outside audit-a large accounting firm like Ernst & Young checking the corporate books on behalf of the shareholders. However, most large companies have an internal-audit group that regularly visits individual company branches and checks the company's accounting systems.

Internal auditors perform the investigative and corrective work that ensures the external auditors don't find anything. The internal-audit group reviews the quality of the data, making sure it's both accurate and complete. Internal auditors also evaluate whether the corporate-accounting procedures are effective and universally followed. Finally, internal auditors introduce or revise procedures to improve efficiency and reduce costs.

Divisional financial services. In this area, you work with each division's business team to prepare financial plans, make forecasts, and compare actual financial results to forecasts. You may also evaluate the financial consequences of alternative strategies.

Responsibilities include everything from analyzing new business opportunities to restructuring a business or developing a capital-spending program. The

primary concerns are to find better ways of using company assets, reduce costs, and research ways to develop better forecasts. Financial services evaluates the risks versus potential return of any course of action and develops recommendations so that managers can pick the most profitable strategies, depending on their goals.

Taxes. Activities in this area involve administering taxes (i.e., paying taxes on time—or finding loopholes to avoid paying them) and planning how to decrease the company's tax burden. Responsibilities include working with attorneys on tax litigation, researching tax laws and reporting requirements by nation (if the company is international), and keeping up with new government rules and regulations.

Large companies have an entire department dedicated to recommending methods to minimize the tax impact of any business decision such as a new division launch, a capital-spending plan, or purchasing a new company. Investments and pensions also need to be managed with an eye toward minimizing taxes. The tax department helps structure transactions, makes recommendations on the timing of acquisitions or sales based on what else will be written off that year, and can decide what corporate-reporting structure reduces taxes—for example, creating a wholly owned subsidiary versus having an internal division.

Treasury. The treasury department is responsible for all of a company's financing and investing activities. This department works with investment bankers who help the corporation raise capital with stock or bond sales or expand through mergers and acquisitions. Treasury also manages the pension fund and the corporation's investments in other companies. The department also handles risk management, making sure that the right steps are taken to safeguard corporate assets by using insurance policies or currency hedges.

Cash management. This is a company's piggy bank. The cash-management group makes sure the company has enough cash on hand to meet its daily needs. The group also sees to it that any excess cash is invested overnight by picking the best short-term investment options. And it negotiates with local banks to get regional business units the banking services they need at the best price.

Corporate development and strategic planning. Corporate development involves both corporate finance and business development. Finance experts in corporate development study acquisition targets, investment options, and licensing deals. Often they assess the best firms to buy or invest in, such as pre-IPO cutting-edge technology companies with complementary products that could either extend the company's product line or mitigate a potential future competitor. Corporate development jobs require planning and analysis know-how and the kind of skills that investment bankers working merger-and-acquisition deals put to use.

Additional Resources

CFO.com (http://www.cfo.com)

Investors' Business Daily (http://www.investors.com)

Institutional Investor Online (http://www.institutionalinvestor.com)

Knowledge @ Wharton: Finance and Investment
(http://knowledge.wharton.upenn.edu/category.cfm?catid=1)

McKinsey Quarterly: Financial Services
(http://www.mckinseyquarterly.com/category_editor.asp?L2=10)

Ohio State University List of Finance Site
(http://www.cob.ohio-state.edu/fin/journal/jofsites.htm)

Careers

General Management

Career Overview

General managers (GMs), also known as executives, or the executive team, run a company's business. They include the chief executive officer (CEO), chief operating officer (COO), president, and others. Their knowledge about an industry and their ability to provide direction can mean the difference between an organization's success and failure. They are involved in planning and policy making at almost every level, including both the long-term strategy and its day-to-day execution.

A GM decides what products to produce, which markets to go after, and the company's general philosophy. GMs are also expected to raise money, keep a company profitable, and answer to shareholders.

GMs also need to be their companies' biggest advocates. They communicate the value of their organizations to the outside world. Employees, strategic partners, shareholders, and even a company's chairperson rely on the general management team to promote the company's interests at every turn. GMs give their subordinates a reason to want to work for them. They instill a sense of pride in shareholders.

General managers tell the press why people should care about their products, marketing strategy, and goals. Without their guidance a company could flounder. General managers bring a measure of order and purpose to their organizations.

Small businesses and start-ups often have limited management teams. The founders, who take on the titles of CEO and president, typically lead such companies. As a company grows and departmentalizes, the general management function is divided into a family of positions.

While the CEO and president remain committed to the overall mission of the organization, other positions have more specialized responsibilities. Some examples are the chief operations officer (COO), chief financial officer (CFO), chief technical officer (CTO), and general manager (GM). Underneath them are department heads who run specific areas of an organization, such as marketing or human resources. They in turn hire and oversee managers who handle the day-to-day supervision of lower-level employees.

In this way, larger corporations have developed a well-defined chain of command. Lower-level employees answer to operational managers, who oversee their daily work. Many firms have several layers of frontline and middle managers. Such supervisors are responsible for managing the functions of an organization. They set project goals, make hiring decisions, settle staff disputes, and ensure that deadlines are met.

Operational managers report to department heads who set policy and determine the goals of their divisions. Department heads answer to the executive officer who controls their area of specialty. For example, the heads of Web development and information technology answer to the CTO.

Executive officers work together to set the goals and policies of a corporation. Their work is overseen by the general manager or president, who supervises the entire organization. Above them is the CEO, the highest-ranking manager. The CEO is held accountable for all aspects of the business. However, the CEO still has to answer to the board of directors.

In publicly held corporations, the board is ultimately responsible for the success of an organization. Members of the board have a fiduciary responsibility to look after the stockholders' (owners') interests first and foremost. If the company begins to falter, they have the right and the duty to correct the situation using any means possible, up to and including firing the CEO or any other top executive. In some cases, the board takes control of all managerial functions until a business has stabilized.

GMs can be found in every industry and organization, from publicly held companies to nonprofits and governmental agencies. Before entering management, GMs should have first proven themselves in their core industries. Usually they work for a while as operations managers, then slowly work their way up the corporate ladder.

Requirements

GMs must have significant experience in both industry and management. Quite a few have consulting experience at a top-tier strategy firm. An MBA or other advanced degree from an Ivy League or top-ten school can improve your chances of being offered a GM position.

Successful general managers have a lot in common. They are inevitably charismatic leaders who inspire their employees to reach their highest potential. They have developed strong written and oral communication skills, a flair for public speaking, the ability to make others feel at ease, and a strong, focused sense of purpose. Furthermore, they know how to get things done and aren't afraid to rock the boat to do so.

Long hours and extended travel are expected. Many GMs are on the road more than 90 percent of the time, visiting national and international offices, attending meetings and conferences sponsored by associations, monitoring operations, meeting with customers, and attending trade shows.

Career Tracks

The responsibilities of those in general management vary depending on the size and type of the organization involved. Smaller companies and start-ups usually have a few key GMs. As an organization grows and diversifies, general management duties will be broken up into a family of positions, which become increasingly specialized as the business grows larger. The following are descriptions of positions you can find in most publicly traded companies.

Chief executive officer (CEO). A CEO is the highest-ranking manager in a company. Most are offered near-total autonomy in handling the day-to-day affairs of their organizations. All staff members work under their authority.

CEOs of publicly traded companies must answer to a board of directors. The board sets the standards by which a CEO must live. Board members can order a CEO's dismissal if they feel that he or she is not meeting the objectives they've set.

A CEO has to have a clear vision for the future of the company, then express that plan to employees, shareholders, and business partners, inspiring them all with confidence. CEOs must be able to raise money by getting venture capitalists to buy into their dreams, or Wall Street to underwrite a bond offering worth hundreds of millions of dollars. When necessary, CEOs will ruffle feathers. They know how to get things done and are willing to do whatever it takes.

Some CEOs are more involved in their companies than others. In small organizations, the CEO may be part of day-to-day operations. Other CEOs concentrate on promoting their companies by giving speeches, attending trade shows, cultivating the press, and acting as evangelists for their companies. They leave the direct management work to the president and general manager.

President. Working directly under the CEO, the president manages the daily operations of a company. While the CEO is the organization's superstar, the president works behind the scenes to make sure nothing gets bogged down in operations. He or she understands the corporate structure, how the industry is shaped, and what the primary objectives of the company are. The president interprets the vision expressed by the CEO and puts it into language that can be followed by everyone within the organization. Most of the president's time is spent working with other executive officers, particularly the COO. Together they ensure that the company's main goals are being achieved. The president's job is demanding and full of pressure. Those who succeed in it are often promoted to the CEO level.

Chief operations officer (COO). The COO works directly under the president and CEO. His or her primary job responsibility is to oversee department heads and other key executives. Together they establish the operational policies for an organization. The COO makes sure everything runs smoothly. As needed, he or she provides reports on operational functions.

While the chief operations officer's role is crucial, it is not one that receives a lot of press. As long as operations go as expected, the COO is left to his or her own devices. Successful COOs can be promoted to president or CEO.

General manager. General managers fill a role similar to that of the president and COO. Typically, GMs work for manufacturing companies and oversee their day-to-day operations. They spend most of their time in the office, working with department heads and other chief executives. Their primary function is to understand how their businesses operate and how to achieve or maintain their long-term economic viability. GMs analyze financial data and are responsible for producing profit and loss statements. They directly oversee the product development, operations, finance, sales, marketing, and purchasing departments. GMs answer directly to the president, or possibly the CEO, and are often first in line for such positions if they become available.

Most GMs are seasoned managers with strong financial backgrounds. They may have worked at various positions within their organizations. At the very least, potential applicants must have significant industry experience. As with any other executive position, general managers are expected to perform at all times. Any decline in profits can lead to their termination.

Chief financial officer (CFO). The CFO is responsible for managing and analyzing all the financial resources of an organization. He or she works with the CEO and other chief executives to plan and implement strategies that will maintain the company's success. CFOs determine how much capital their companies need to have on hand to operate properly. They also reinvest corporate profits in safe but lucrative business opportunities. Some other possible responsibilities include raising capital, acquiring or merging with other businesses, taking a company public, and analyzing changing tax laws.

CFOs usually have extensive accounting and finance backgrounds. They are detail oriented and highly analytical. Possible promotion opportunities include becoming a COO, general manager, or president.

Chief technology officer (CTO). CTOs develop an organization's short- and long-term information technology goals. A CTO must keep abreast of technological developments in his or her industry, develop technology-related product strategies, evaluate development options, establish strategic partnerships, negotiate licensing arrangements, and manage all intellectual property-related matters. A CTO works with a CFO and COO to determine which technologies meet the needs of employees without breaking a company's budget.

Besides having a strong technical background, the CTO must be an accomplished manager. The most important skill for CTOs is the ability to analyze changing technologies and predict how future advances will affect a company's business model.

Board of directors. While board members are not technically on staff, they are ultimately responsible for maintaining the value of a company. Most boards are made up of major shareholders, founding partners, industry experts, and venture capitalists. Members of the board of directors act to protect the financial interests of shareholders. The board meets periodically with the CEO to go over key business strategies. Board members offer advice, ask the hard questions, and refuse to accept anything less than success.

If board members think the CEO or another chief executive is not living up to his or her potential, they retain the right to fire that executive. If a company begins to falter, the board may step in and take over all managerial functions. The board has total control over hiring a CEO and may insist on helping select other key executives.

Additional Resources

American Management Association (http://www.amanet.org/index.htm)

BRINT.com (http://www.brint.com)

ExecuNet
(http://www.execunet.com/execmeta/index.cfm?&CFID=1205345&CFTOKE
N=2847483)

McKinsey Quarterly: Organization
(http://www.mckinseyquarterly.com/category_editor.asp?L2=18)

McKinsey Quarterly: Strategy
(http://www.mckinseyquarterly.com/category_editor.asp?L2=21)

Investment Banking

Career Overview

The intensely competitive, action-oriented, profit-hungry world of investment banking can seem like a bigger-than-life place where deals are done and fortunes are made. In fact, it's a great place to learn the ins and outs of corporate finance and pick up analytical skills that will remain useful throughout your business career. But investment banking has a very steep learning curve, and chances are you'll start off in a job whose duties are more *Working Girl* than *Wall Street*.

Wall Street is filled with high-energy, hardworking young hotshots. Some are investment bankers who spend hours hunched behind computers, poring over financial statements and churning out spreadsheets by the pound. Others are traders who keep one eye on their Bloomberg screen, a phone over each ear, and a buyer or seller on hold every minute the market's in session. Traders work hand in hand with the institutional sales group, whose members hop from airport to airport trying to sell big institutions a piece of the new stock offering they have coming down the pipeline. Then there are the analytically minded research analysts, who read, write, live, and breathe whichever industry they follow, 24/7.

Investment banking isn't one specific service or function. It is an umbrella term for a range of activities: underwriting, selling, and trading securities (stocks and bonds); providing financial advisory services, such as mergers and acquisition advice; and managing assets. Investment banks offer these services to companies, governments, nonprofit institutions, and individuals.

Careers

Traditionally, commercial banks and investment banks performed completely distinct functions. When Joe on Main Street needed a loan to buy a car, he visited a commercial bank. When Sprint needed to raise cash to fund an acquisition or build its fiber-optic network, it called on its investment bank. Paychecks and lifestyles reflected this division too, with investment bankers reveling in their large bonuses and glamorous ways while commercial bankers worked nine-to-five and then went home to their families. Today, as the laws requiring the separation of investment and commercial banking are reformed, more and more firms are making sure they have a foot in both camps, thus blurring the lines and the cultures. The action and players are still centered in New York City and a few other money centers around the world, but the list of players is getting smaller as the industry consolidates. Today, leading banks include Merrill Lynch, Goldman Sachs, Morgan Stanley, Citigroup, Deutsche Bank, Credit Suisse First Boston, and J.P. Morgan Chase. These and other firms are regular visitors to campus career centers.

Investment bankers issue financial products; sell and trade them, invest in them, research them, and advise others on financial transactions. A full-service investment bank includes three major professional divisions: investment banking (which includes corporate finance, mergers and acquisitions, and public finance), sales and trading, and research.

Nearly all banks have a staff of research analysts who study economic trends and news, individual company stocks, and industry developments in order to provide proprietary investment advice to institutional clients and in-house groups, such as the sales and trading divisions. The research division also plays an important role in the underwriting process, both in wooing the client with its knowledge of the client's industry and in providing a link to the institutions that own the client's stock once it's publicly traded. However, in light of recent corporate scandals, in which banks were accused of favorably analyzing who

were investment clients of the bank, there is growing pressure on Wall Street to separate its research and banking functions. This aspect of the industry could look quite different in the next several years.

The corporate finance group (frequently known as "banking" or "CorpFin") serves the sellers of securities. These may be either Fortune 1000 companies looking to raise cash to fund growth or, frequently, private companies wanting to go public (i.e., to sell stock on the public markets for the first time). Think of investment bankers as financial consultants to corporations. This is where CEOs and CFOs turn when they're trying to figure out how to finance their operations, how to structure their balance sheets, or how best to move ahead with plans to sell or acquire a company.

The activities of the CorpFin department can range from providing pure financial advice to leading a company through its first equity issue (or IPO). As a result, industry or product knowledge is key, and many investment banks divide their corporate finance departments into industry subgroups, such as technology, financial institutions, health care, communications, entertainment, utilities, and insurance, or into product groups like high-yield, private equity, and investment-grade debt.

The job of salespeople is to ensure their bank's financial stability by getting investors to commit to buying (subscribing to) stock and bond issues before the new securities actually hit the market. The mergers and acquisitions department provides advice to companies that are buying other companies, or which are being acquired by others.

Careers

Requirements

If you have an MBA or other advanced business certification, you'll be paid more for a position than someone with a fresh BA. But those with prior experience always get first shot, so be sure to get an internship. Industry expertise and prior corporate finance work can also be a way in, but you'll have to be patient.

Career Tracks

While the various groups within an investment bank support each other, the work and responsibilities in each group vary.

Corporate finance. Investment bankers are like financial consultants for corporations—which is precisely where the Corporate Finance Group comes into play. As a member of Banking or CorpFin, you serve the sellers of securities—Fortune 1000 companies in need of cash to fund growth, and private companies that are looking to complete an IPO—by buying all the shares or all the bonds a company has for sale, which are then resold by your firm's sales force to investors on the market.

Many investment banks divide their corporate finance departments into industry subgroups, such as technology, financial institutions, health care, communications, entertainment, utilities, and insurance, or into product groups such as high-yield, private equity, and investment-grade debt.

As an investment banker in corporate finance, you will underwrite equity and debt (bond) offerings, help firms devise and implement financial strategies, analyze their financial needs (such as how to structure balance sheets and when and how to proceed with funding initiatives), and work with the sales and trading departments to determine valuations for new offerings.

Mergers and acquisitions. The mergers and acquisitions group (known as M&A) provides advice to companies that are buying another company or are themselves being acquired. M&A work can seem very glamorous and high-profile. At the same time, the work leading up to the headline-grabbing multibillion-dollar acquisition can involve a herculean effort to crunch all the numbers, perform the necessary due diligence, and work out the complicated structure of the deal. As one insider puts it, "You have to really like spending time in front of your computer with Excel." Often, the M&A team will also work with a CorpFin industry group to arrange the appropriate financing for the transaction (usually a debt or equity offering). In many cases, all this may happen on a very tight timeline and under extreme secrecy. M&A is often a subgroup within corporate finance; but in some firms, it is a stand-alone department. M&A can be one of the most demanding groups to work for.

Public finance. Public finance is similar to corporate finance except that instead of dealing with corporations, it works with public entities such as city and state governments and agencies, bridge and airport authorities, housing authorities, hospitals, and the like. Although the basic services (financial advisory and underwriting) and the financial tools (bonds and swaps, but no equity) are similar to those used for private-sector clients, numerous political and regulatory considerations must be assessed in the structuring of each deal. A particular key issue involves how to get and maintain tax-exempt status for the financial instruments the client will use.

Sales and traders sell and trade securities. Read the career profile on securities sales and trading for more on what they do.

Research. Research departments are generally divided into two main groups: fixed-income research and equity research. Both types of research can incorporate several different efforts, including quantitative research (corporate-

financing strategies, specific product development, and pricing models), economic research (economic analysis and forecasts of U.S. and international economic trends, interest rates, and currency movement), and individual company research. It's important to understand that these are "sell-side" analysts (because they in effect "sell" or market stocks to investors), rather than the "buy-side" analysts who work for the institutional investors themselves.

As a researcher, you'll meet with company management and analyze a company's financial statements and operations, provide written and oral updates on market trends and company performance, attend or organize industry conferences, speak with the sales force, traders, and investment bankers about company or industry trends, develop proprietary pricing models for financial products, make presentations to clients on relevant market trends and economic data, offer forecasts and recommendations, and watch emerging companies.

Additional Resources

InvestorLinks.com (http://www.investorlinks.com)

SNL Financial (http://www.snl.com)

The Motley Fool (http://www.fool.com)

Wall Street Journal (http://online.wsj.com/public/us)

Marketing

Career Overview

Broadly speaking, marketing is the intermediary function between product development and sales. In a nutshell, it's the marketer's job to ensure that consumers look beyond price and functionality when they're weighing consumption options.

Marketers create, manage, and enhance brands. (A brand can be thought of as the way consumers perceive a particular company or its products and how a company reinforces or enhances those perceptions through its overall communications—its logo, advertising, packaging, etc.) Marketers want the consumer to ask: "Which brand helps me look and feel my best? Which brand can I trust?" Their goal is to make the brand they represent the obvious and uncontested answer to those questions in the consumer's mind. In marketing terms, this is called owning share of mind.

Of course, a brand can't be all things to all people. A key part of a marketer's job is to understand the needs, preferences, and constraints that define the target group of consumers (who may be from the same geographic region, income level, age range, lifestyle, or interest group) or the market niche corresponding to the brand. How can a company aggressively expand its market share and keep customers satisfied? That question is central to everything a marketer does.

Marketing is a function at every company in every industry. In the consumer products industry, marketing (called *brand management*) is the lead function. In other industries marketing may play a supporting role to another function. At a high-tech company, for instance, marketing may play a supporting role to research and development. And in advertising, market research, and public relations, a specialized marketing function is the industry.

Requirements

Marketing people come from many different academic backgrounds, but certain backgrounds will help more than others.

If you're interested in getting into brand management or market research, an education that includes courses in business, economics, or statistics will serve you better than a liberal arts major will. A marketing career of any kind requires a sharp, analytical mind; strong oral and written communication skills; and a keen interest in business and consumer behavior.

The best way to get into marketing, regardless of what you've studied, is by taking an internship. Many PR firms, ad agencies, and high-tech and Internet companies offer marketing internships. Unless you're enrolled in an MBA program, internships are harder to come by at consumer-products companies.

The large consumer-products companies recruit at select schools, and the best way to get hired by one of them is through on-campus recruiting. For PR, advertising, and marketing positions in other industries, your best bet may be to network or to contact firms directly.

Career Tracks

Some companies define marketing positions broadly, encompassing everything from market research and strategy to advertising, promotions, and public relations. Other companies have large marketing departments, with marketers dedicated to one of these roles. And still other companies contract out many marketing functions to firms that specialize in advertising, public relations, and market research.

What follows are descriptions of some common marketing roles.

Market research. For a company to capture a market, it first must understand that market. Whether the intended target for the product is individual consumers or businesses, the company must know what motivates consumers, what their needs and purchasing habits are, and how they view themselves in relation to the rest of the world.

Market researchers use surveys, studies, and focus groups to collect data on a brand's target. Some companies have their own market-research divisions. Others hire specialized firms to conduct research for them. Ideally, market researchers should have both qualitative and quantitative analytical ability because their job depends on gathering data from human subjects, besides crunching numbers and interpreting the results.

Brand management. Brand management is the key function in the consumer products industry. Traditionally considered the best training ground for people interested in long-term marketing careers, leading consumer-products companies such as Procter & Gamble, Clorox, and General Mills are often compared to Ivy League colleges because of their rigorous admission standards and strong training programs.

Brand managers assume responsibility for a brand or a brand family. They might be likened to small business owners, but that isn't an accurate comparison because they rarely need to get their hands dirty in day-to-day operations. Instead, they focus on the big picture: distilling the brand's essence, mapping out the competitive landscape in the brand's category, identifying market opportunities, and communicating (through a public relations agency or advertising firm) the unique benefits the product delivers to consumers.

Although they usually don't undertake heavy-duty research themselves, brand managers guide market-research studies by setting the agenda and criteria and by choosing stimuli, such as product-benefit statements, pictures, product samples, and video clips. Once the research is complete, brand managers analyze the data that's been collected and develop a marketing strategy—a short-term business plan for the brand.

The strategy may call for a new ad campaign or new products or it may outline a bold new vision for the brand. Brand managers then ensure that other functions (promotions, market research, research and development, and manufacturing) are working in concert to implement the strategy they've articulated.

Promotions. Companies in which marketing is a particularly strong function may have a dedicated promotions staff to create programs that unite advertising to purchasing incentives such as coupons, special discounts, samples, gifts, rebates, or sweepstakes. To promote its promotions, the staff may use direct mail, telemarketing, advertisements, in-store displays, product endorsements, or special events.

Public relations. Public relations personnel manage communications with the media, consumers, employees, investors, or the general public. They are the spokespeople for their own company or for client companies, if they work for a public relations firm. They may write press releases to promote new products or to inform the investment community of financial results, business partnerships, or other organizational news. If they're in media relations, they may respond to information requests from journalists, pitch stories to the media, or even ghostwrite op-ed pieces about the company.

In general, the goal of the public relations specialist is to portray the company in a flattering light, publicize its products and services, uphold its public image in a crisis, and generate positive buzz around its business and corporate practices.

Additional Resources

BrandWeek (http://www.brandweek.com/brandweek/index.jsp)

Knowledge @ Wharton: Marketing
(http://knowledge.wharton.upenn.edu/category.cfm?catid=4)

MarketingPower.com (http://www.marketingpower.com)

McKinsey Quarterly: Marketing
(http://www.mckinseyquarterly.com/category_editor.asp?L2=16)

ProductScan Online (http://www.productscan.com)

Operations

Career Overview

The operations team creates the infrastructure of a company. Operations employees help determine where an organization should be based, its employment policies, accounting practices, distribution channels, and much more. While individual departments determine how corporate procedures are implemented, operations makes sure they are designed optimally in the first place.

The chief operations officer is a senior member in most organizations. The COO works with the CEO and company president to determine the company's vision. Their ideas are filtered down through the rest of the company.

Senior operations managers determine where an organization is based, what its facilities will look like, which vendors to use, and how the hiring policy will be implemented. Once the key decisions are made, lower-level operations personnel carry them out.

Accountants and controllers watch the books. Administrators and managers supervise line employees. Sales reps and customer service agents ensure clients get what they've paid for. If a problem exists, operations personnel will be the first to hear about it. They work to find a solution, and then set about fixing the problem.

While operations is a key component of any successful company, it is back-end work. Most support functions fall under operations' control. Such functions include customer service, logistics, production, maintenance, and administration.

Sometimes, depending on the size and scope of an organization, operations will also include sales, accounting, programming, and marketing. The goal of the operations department is to find solutions to problems before they affect the bottom line.

Requirements

While you can get a customer service job with little experience, most operations positions require a four-year degree and at least some industry background. Most universities offer degrees in operations management. But a degree in business, accounting, or administration is just as good. Most employees who work at lower-level operations positions will work their way up the corporate ladder. An operations assistant could be made an operations manager within a year or two.

If you are interested in climbing the corporate ladder, you should consider getting an advanced degree.

Most VPs and COOs have an MBA, and many have a PhD. Without such degrees, promotions to higher levels will take a lot longer. It may also be more difficult to land a job at another organization.

To be promoted, an individual must prove he or she can be a good supervisor, get a job done right the first time, manage all aspects of a project, and keep it within budget parameters. A detail-oriented personality, strong analytical skills, and the ability to thrive in a team environment are necessities.

Career Tracks

The operations department is responsible for ensuring a company operates as efficiently and economically as possible. Exactly which functions it controls depends on the size and structure of the organization.

What follows are common operations-related positions you can find at Internet companies, though such positions have equivalents throughout other industries.

Controller. The controller watches out for the financial well-being of an organization. He or she manages the books, creates profit and loss statements, keeps projects within budget parameters, and prepares financial reports. Controllers work closely with operations managers and other accounting personnel. A strong financial background, an understanding of business processes, and a detail-oriented nature are prerequisites.

Facilities coordinator. Facilities coordinators design the physical environment of an organization. The facilities coordinator is interested in how a building's design, layout, furniture, and other equipment affect the efficiency and profitability of the business that uses them.

The facilities coordinator will buy office furniture and supplies, determine when more space is needed, select appropriate vendors, and be responsible for the facilities budget. Besides having a business management background, the facilities coordinator needs to have a keen understanding of how working environments affect employee productivity.

Logistics engineer. A business needs to plan how work orders will be distributed throughout its organization. The logistics engineer is the person primarily responsible for such planning. He or she is interested in improving the efficiency and accuracy of order fulfillment, and will map out the process

from beginning to end, always on the lookout for possible improvements. This is a detail-oriented position that requires strong problem-solving skills and an in-depth analysis of business processes.

Project manager. Most projects will have a single leader who watches over them from beginning to end. The essential role of the project manager is to establish group goals. He or she will also supervise the work of lower-level staff, ensure deadlines are met, put in requests for additional supplies and staff, and keep a particular project on time and under budget. In most cases, the project manager will answer to the operations manager.

Operations analyst. An operations analyst analyzes how the current operations infrastructure is working. He or she attempts to find areas where the system breaks down, and then finds ways to improve it. Strategies may include changing the work environment, changing employment policies, using different vendors, or changing the process. There is a great deal of administrative work involved. This position answers to the operations manager.

Operations manager/director. The operations manager or director watches over his or her department, the size and scope of which depends on the organization involved. A large company may have several operations managers. Their job is to determine how the processes in their departments should be implemented and what duties need to be performed.

An operations manager also hires and manages lower-level staff, selects the vendors, completes departmental financial analyses, and determines the budget. The operations manager reports to the VP of operations or chief operating officer (COO).

Chief operations officer (COO). One of the senior managers in any business organization, the chief operations officer is responsible for making sure that the entire back end of an organization operates as efficiently as possible. (The general management career profile has more about senior management roles.) The chief operations officer could be responsible for marketing, programming, customer support, sales, accounting, distribution, legal, or just about any other business function you could think of.

While the CEO is supposed to be the visionary for a company, the COO is a company's administrator. Without his or her involvement, a company could fail. The COO is a seasoned professional with many years' experience. He or she reports to a company's CEO and board of directors.

Additional Resources

BRINT.com (http://www.brint.com)

McKinsey Quarterly: Operations
(http://www.mckinseyquarterly.com/category_editor.asp?L2=1)

McKinsey Quarterly: Organization
(http://www.mckinseyquarterly.com/category_editor.asp?L2=18)

Careers

Project Management

Career Overview

Everyone practices project management to some degree. A writer blocks out her novel, homeowners plan their housework, the host of a dinner party makes sure the meal is served on time.

In business, project management is an art, a skill, and a demanding full-time job. Project managers (PMs) are key employees in such industries as construction, engineering, architecture, manufacturing, and real estate development, but many opportunities for PMs exist outside these areas. In computer hardware and software for example, project managers are responsible for launching new products, developing new technologies, and managing alliance programs with strategic partners.

Large corporations such as insurance companies and bank may also hire PMs to manage the implementation of new standards or practices in their many branch offices. Internet companies often look for project managers to oversee site launches or the development of new applications.

Whether a project involves constructing a building, releasing a product, or launching a rocket, project managers make sure everything comes together in a timely, cost-effective manner—and take the heat if it doesn't. Their high-profile, high-risk work demands multitasking ability, analytical thinking, and excellent communication skills.

Project managers live and breathe by their schedules. In most cases, a project is planned down to the daily or even hourly level, and a formal schedule is developed using the Critical Path Method (CPM), a precedence-based technique that determines the sequence in which things must happen. Milestones punctuate most project schedules, indicating the required completion of various steps.

Most scheduling programs also help allocate resources, another big part of a project manager's job. If you are running a software development project, for example, you have to know how many engineers will be available and how many hours they'll need to work. Likewise, if you're running a construction project involving cranes and excavators that must be leased on an hourly basis, you'll need to know when to have those machines on site to get the most work done for the least money. Balancing limited labor, materials, and other resources is a difficult task that earns a good project manager top dollar.

Requirements

Educational requirements for project managers vary greatly according to the type of projects they manage. For construction projects, a civil engineering degree is usually required. High-tech PMs may need a degree in electrical engineering or computer science. In all cases, the most successful project managers have some type of formal business training, such as an MBA. Project management has a direct effect on a company's bottom line, so a PM must be able to evaluate a project's financial repercussions from a corporate point of view.

Project managers also need strong leadership skills, the ability to set and stick to a schedule, multitasking ability, analytical thinking, strong communication skills, and an orientation toward getting things done.

Professional certification in project management is available through the Project Management Institute, which bestows the profession's most globally recognized and respected credential—certification as a Project Management Professional. To obtain the PMP credential, applicants must satisfy requirements involving education and experience, agree to a code of ethics, and pass the PMP certification examination. Many corporations require PMP certification for employment or advancement.

Career Tracks

Project manager. In this position, you may run a project yourself or lead a management team, delegating task management to assistants. PMs report to the "owner" of a project—whether that's a real estate developer, a government agency, or your company's senior management. You're not paying the money, but you take responsibility for the project's proper completion.

Senior project manager. Many large organizations that tackle multiple projects at once (especially construction and engineering companies) employ a senior project manager. The senior project manager supervises a company's various project managers, coordinating the allocation of company resources, approving costs, and deciding which projects should take priority.

Additional Resources

Project Manager (http://www.project-manager.com)

Project Management Forum (http://www.pmforum.org)

ProjectManagement.com (http://www.projectmanagement.com/home)

Securities Sales & Trading

Career Overview

Securities sales and trading is where the rubber meets the road in the investment banking industry. An investment bank relies on its sales department to sell bonds or shares of stock in companies it underwrites. Investors who want to buy or sell a certain stock or bond will place an order with a broker or sales representative, who writes the ticket for the order. The trader makes the trade.

Securities sales and trading are high-profile, high-pressure roles in the investment banking industry. Unlike other I-banking careers, such as corporate finance, public finance, and M&A, where the emphasis is on the team, securities salespeople and traders are independent, working on commission to bring to market the financial products that others create.

In the United States, the securities business revolves around markets (also known as "exchanges") such as the New York Stock Exchange, the Chicago Board of Trade, and Nasdaq, where debt, futures, options, stocks, and other financial instruments are bought and sold. Salespeople and traders are independent agents working under a simple contract: The firm provides a place to do business in return for a percentage of the business that salespeople and traders generate.

Salespeople are called brokers or dealers. As one of them, you're expected to build a "book" of clients. No matter how long you've been working, and no matter how many clients you have, you're expected to cold call. New brokers make as many as 600 cold calls a day. Most of the work takes place over the

Careers

telephone: soliciting clients or selling a particular stock or bond issue. You'll use analyst research and every sales trick in the book to push your securities to investors.

Traders make money by trading securities. Although they're the ones who transact trades for the brokers and their clients, traders are primarily responsible for taking a position in a security issue, and buying or selling large amounts of stocks or bonds using an employer's (or their own) capital. When they bet right, they win big; when they bet wrong, they lose big.

Brokers and traders build their lives around market hours. On the West Coast, you'll start working before 6:00 a.m., so that you're ready to go when the opening bell rings. There's no flextime, no long coffee breaks, and no time to run errands.

Requirements

There are no hard and fast educational or professional prerequisites for selling securities. However, the National Association of Securities Dealers (NASD) and the Securities and Exchange Commission (SEC) require brokers to get licenses, depending on a particular broker's role:

- You'll need to pass the Series 7 General Security Sales License exam to sell most types of securities.
- Individuals who wish to sell commodities or futures contracts must pass the Series 3 exam.
- Most brokers also need to pass a Series 63 License exam, dealing with state laws regarding securities sales.
- Managers need the Series 8 License for general sales supervisors in order to manage branch activities.
- Managers supervising options sales personnel or compliance need to pass the Series 4 License exam.

Would-be salespeople must also pass a background check to make sure they have no criminal history that would preclude them from being an "honest" broker.

Aside from the background and license checks, branch managers hire salespeople based on evaluations of candidates' ability to think on their feet, communicate effectively, deal with numbers, and, above all, make cold calls. Traders can break in by assisting other traders on the floor and starting trading accounts.

Image means a great deal in sales and trading: How you dress, how you carry yourself, and how you act will be as impressive to a securities sales manager as your educational or professional background. If you have experience in sales, that's a plus, but a manager is really looking for people who will put in the hours, make the calls, and generate revenue. And as in all areas of financial services, networking is key. Scour your alma mater's alumni connections, pester your friends and relatives, and follow any lead that might get your foot in the door.

Career Tracks

In securities sales and trading, you're in business for yourself. If you are a sales representative, your career track will consist of building your business, or book, to the point where you have a substantial number of clients for whom you trade. If you're a trader, your career track will consist of trading financial instruments (stocks, bonds, and other securities).

As with securities sales, the job of the trader doesn't change over time; traders get sharper, develop better instincts, and benefit from experience as they go along. Due to the pressure of the career, few last to middle age.

If you're interested in trading, check out internship opportunities. Many firms offer summer positions to outstanding students, providing candidates with much-needed experience and connections. Check out a company's website to research its internship offerings.

Securities sales representative (broker). Securities sales representatives—or brokers—act as intermediaries between buyers and sellers, and they make money off of commissions. In some cases, such as when trading stocks, bonds, and options, they need to be registered as agents of an investment house. Brokers give advice to customers and then make deals happen. Usually they specialize in a particular type of security, such as futures, options, or bonds.

Those who do well make a lot of money and may get a larger office and an assistant, but the work remains fundamentally the same. Brokers are sometimes called dealers, investment advisers, investment counselors, or investment representatives, but the work is the same.

Branch manager. Senior sales representatives who have proven themselves on the trading floor may become branch managers. Branch managers hire salespeople, fire those who don't do well, and make sure that brokers meet sales and revenue targets. While branch managers make additional income in the form of commission overrides (a percentage of the commissions made by the brokers working under them), they're responsible not just for their sales, but their office totals.

Floor trader. Floor traders run around the floor of an exchange (e.g., the NYSE), swapping tickets and making trades. Floor traders are responsible for locating the buyers and connecting them with the sellers (or connecting the sellers with the buyers). As prices change quickly in a turbulent market, traders are under constant pressure to get deals executed at the prices their clients (or their employers) specify. If a trader can't find somebody to buy or sell at a specified price, the buy or sell order won't go through, and nobody profits: not the buyer, not the seller, and not the trader (or the trader's employer), because there's no commission. Traders work during an exchange's hours of operation, usually without breaks.

Careers

Desk trader. Nasdaq is what might be called a "virtual" stock exchange, as there is no physical building where traders meet to make deals with each other. Brokers have a "Nasdaq desk," which means they can trade on Nasdaq. That desk is actually a bank of traders, all staring intently at their computer screens to see how the market is shaping up, speaking into several phones at once in a mad rush to find buyers or sellers whom brokers or online investors have requested. (Trades made through an online account, such as at Charles Schwab or TD Waterhouse, go directly to the trader, bypassing the broker.)

Additional Resources

Investors' Business Daily (http://www.investors.com)

Institutional Investor Online (http://www.institutionalinvestor.com)

Knowledge @ Wharton: Finance and Investment
(http://knowledge.wharton.upenn.edu/category.cfm?catid=1)

McKinsey Quarterly: Financial Services
(http://www.mckinseyquarterly.com/category_editor.asp?L2=10)

National Association of Securities Dealers (http://www.nasd.com)

Ohio State University List of Finance Sites
(http://www.cob.ohio-state.edu/fin/journal/jofsites.htm)

WetFeet's Insider Guide Series

Ace Your Case! The WetFeet Insider Guide to Consulting Interviews
Ace Your Case II: Fifteen More Consulting Cases
Ace Your Case III: Practice Makes Perfect
Ace Your Case IV: The Latest and Greatest
Ace Your Interview! The WetFeet Insider Guide to Interviewing
Beat the Street: The WetFeet Insider Guide to Investment Banking Interviews
Getting Your Ideal Internship
Get Your Foot in the Door! Landing the Job Interview
Job Hunting A to Z: The WetFeet Insider Guide to Landing the Job You Want
Killer Consulting Resumes!
Killer Cover Letters and Resumes!
Killer Investment Banking Resumes!
Negotiating Your Salary and Perks
Networking Works!: The WetFeet Insider Guide to Networking

Career and Industry Guides

Accounting
Advertising and Public Relations
Asset Management and Retail Brokerage
Biotech and Pharmaceuticals
Brand Management
Health Care
Human Resources
Computer Software and Hardware
Consulting for Ph.D.s, Lawyers, and Doctors
Industries and Careers for MBAs
Industries and Careers for Undergrads
Information Technology
Investment Banking

Management Consulting
Marketing and Market Research
Non-Profits and Government Agencies
Oil and Gas
Real Estate
Sports and Entertainment
Top 20 Biotechnology and Pharmaceutical Firms
Top 25 Consulting Firms
Top 25 Financial Services Firms
Top 20 Law Firms
Venture Capital

Company Guides

Accenture
Bain & Company
Bear Stearns
Booz Allen Hamilton
The Boston Consulting Group
Cap Gemini Ernst & Young
Citigroup
Credit Suisse First Boston
Deloitte Consulting
Goldman Sachs
IBM Business Consulting Services
JPMorgan Chase
Lehman Brothers
McKinsey & Company
Merrill Lynch
Monitor Group
Morgan Stanley